The Delany Sisters' Book of Everyday Wisdom

G·K
Hall
&Co.

Also published in Large Print from
G.K. Hall by Sarah and A. Elizabeth
Delany and Amy Hill Hearth:

*Having Our Say: The Delany Sisters'
First 100 Years*

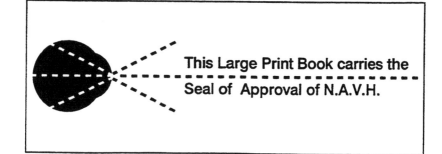

This Large Print Book carries the
Seal of Approval of N.A.V.H.

The Delany Sisters'

Book of
Everyday Wisdom

Sarah and
A. Elizabeth Delany
with
Amy Hill Hearth

G.K. Hall & Co.
Thorndike, Maine

Published in 1995 by arrangement with Kodansha America, Inc.

G.K. Hall Large Print Inspirational Collection.

The text of this Large Print edition is unabridged.
Other aspects of the book may vary from the original edition.

Set in 20 pt. News Plantin.

Printed in the United States on permanent paper.

Library of Congress Cataloging in Publication Data

Delany, Sarah Louise, 1889–
    The Delany sisters' book of everyday wisdom / Sarah and A. Elizabeth Delany, with Amy Hill Hearth.
        p.   cm.
    ISBN 0-7838-1198-5 (lg. print : hc)
    1. Delany, Sarah Louise, 1889– — Quotations. 2. Delany, Annie Elizabeth, 1891– — Quotations. 3. Life skills — Handbooks, manuals, etc. 4. Conduct of life — Quotations, maxims, etc. 5. Afro-Americans — Life skills guides — Quotations, maxims, etc. 6. Large type books. I. Delany, Annie Elizabeth, 1891– . II. Hearth, Amy Hill, 1958-
III. Title.
[E185.96.D368   1995]
973'.00496073'00922—dc20   94-43787

Dedicated to Our Sisters
Julia Delany Bourne (1893–1974)
Laura Delany Murrell (1903–1993)
Helen Hill Kotzky

CONTENTS

ACKNOWLEDGMENTS

The authors would like to thank Daniel A. Strone, Blair A. Hearth, Minato Asakawa, Paul De Angelis, Gillian Jolis, and Trigg Robinson for their advice and support in creating this book; Denise Landis for reviewing the recipes; and Elisa Petrini for friendly words.

PREFACE

"It's as if we've become America's grandmas," Sadie Delany said with a huge smile as we looked through a new basketful of fan mail. Now 105 years old, Sadie Delany, along with her "little" sister Bessie, 103, have become everyone's favorite centenarians.

Charming, candid, and oh-so-wise, the Delany sisters struck a chord in 1993 with their critically acclaimed memoir, *Having Our Say: The Delany Sisters' First 100 Years.* ("Twenty-eight weeks on *The New York Times* best-seller list — not bad for two old inky-dinks over one hundred years old!" Bessie Delany is fond of joking.)

People often ask me if the sisters have changed (or been spoiled) from all of the attention. The answer, quite simply, is not one bit! What can you say about two celebrities who still insist on making their own soap and whose main preoccupation is getting into Heaven?

Their lifestyle, too, has changed little. They still live together in their own home in Mt. Vernon, New York. Great effort has been made to protect their privacy. Yet while the sisters enjoy living quietly, they have thoroughly enjoyed the excitement created by the success of *Having Our Say*. "We've had a ball," Bessie likes to say. And the Delany sisters are thrilled, yet overwhelmed, by the mail they've received.

When the letters came pouring in from readers, they often came with questions. People wanted advice, direction, and encouragement. The way they were raised, the sisters believed they had to answer each and every letter. But what to do? If they lived thirty more years, they would not be able to answer them all.

One day it occurred to the Delany sisters that in lieu of answering the fan mail, we could do another book together. Only this time we would not tell the story of the sisters' lives, but the secrets of old age.

Fortunately, I had kept a journal during the past few years, where I had jotted down the words of advice, parables, and amusing anecdotes that the sisters had passed on to me. We used my journal as a framework, expanding on the entries. Additionally, during the spring and summer of 1994, I prompted the sisters for new thoughts and ideas and wrote them down. As in *Having Our Say*, the sequence of material in the final manuscript is mine, but the words are all theirs.

— AMY HILL HEARTH
Westchester County, New York
September 1994

PROLOGUE

We are the children of a slave. There aren't too many of us left these days.

We were born more than 100 years ago and have lived together all of our lives. Our father, Henry B. Delany, was born a slave on a plantation in Georgia in the year 1858. He met our mama, Miss Nanny Logan, while they were attending Saint Augustine's, a school for Negroes in Raleigh, North Carolina. Mama was an issue-free Negro, which meant she was born free.

Mama and Papa were married at the chapel at Saint Aug's back in 1886 and brought up all ten of us children right on the campus. Papa was an Episcopal priest who served as vice principal of the school (they wouldn't let him be principal because he was a Negro). Mama taught cooking and served as the matron of the school — she ran the day-to-day operations. Papa eventually became the first elected Negro bishop of the Episcopal Church in America.

We didn't have one penny — not one penny — when we were growing up, but we had a blessed childhood. We had a good time, though we were very sheltered. In those days, colored girls couldn't go anywhere without a chaperone. Something bad could happen to you and there wasn't a thing your papa could do about it.

We remember life before Jim Crow Laws were passed in Raleigh in the 1890s. White folks and Negroes mixed together kind of naturally before that. But some nasty white folks — we used to call them "rebby boys," which is probably short for "rebel" — managed to get these Jim Crow Laws passed that set colored folks back a million years. You couldn't use the white folks' library. You had to sit in the *back* of the trolley. You couldn't use the white folks' restroom, which was the one that was kept clean.

God was the center of our Christian home. We had prayers morning and evening, and every night before Mama bathed us, we'd go into Papa's study and he'd read to us from the Bible.

After religion and family life, the most important thing in our lives was education. Back in the 1890s, colored children did not get much chance for an education. Since we grew up on the campus of Saint Aug's, we had a big advantage. At that time, Saint Aug's was a school for teachers and ministers. Because our papa was vice principal, we even got to take some of the classes that were meant for the ministers — like Greek and Latin!

When we graduated from Saint Aug's (Sadie in 1910 and Bessie in 1911), our degree was the equivalent of two years of college today. We were qualified to teach school, but Papa gave us this big speech about getting a four-year degree. He said, "Daughters, you are college material. You owe it to your nation, your race, and yourself to

17

go. And if you don't, then shame on you!"

The only problem was that Papa had no money. And he insisted that we not take scholarships, because he said we'd be beholden to the folks who gave us the money. So what we had to do was pay our own way.

Now that was a mighty big task, but we set out to do it. Both of us worked as teachers down South for eight years until we had enough money to move to New York City and enroll at Columbia University. We each earned advanced degrees (Sadie in education and Bessie in dental surgery). Meanwhile, all but one of our sisters and brothers moved to New York, too. Lemuel, a physician, stayed behind.

Like a lot of Negroes around the time of the First World War, we were moving north in search of opportunity. There was so much racial prejudice in the South that we could not advance ourselves the way we wished. New York was far from perfect, but it was better.

We settled in Harlem, which was a

beehive of activity. During the 1920s and early 1930s, it was the home of what they called the Harlem Renaissance: There were famous writers like Langston Hughes and musicians like Duke Ellington. The movers and shakers of Negro America, like Dr. W.E.B. Du Bois, the great Negro intellectual, all walked the streets of Harlem.

You couldn't help but mingle with these folks. And in the middle of it all were the Delanys!

Our brother Hap was also a dentist, and he and Bessie shared an office at the corner of Seventh Avenue and 135th Street, which became one of the hot gathering spots in Harlem. One of Bessie's patients was James Weldon Johnson, the first executive secretary of the National Association for the Advancement of Colored People (NAACP). Our brothers Lucius and Hubert were attorneys; Hubert was an assistant U.S. district attorney and, eventually, a judge. There were also our two sisters, Julia, a graduate of The Juilliard School of Music, and Laura, a teacher who graduated from Hunter College. And there was Manross, who was a career army man and businessman, and the baby, Sam, who owned a well-known funeral parlor.

They used to say in Harlem that the Delanys could take care of you from cradle to grave: We could take care of your health, teach you how to read and write, serve as your lawyer, and last, but not least, bury you!

Neither of us ever married and the reason is that we picked careers over men. You see, in our day it didn't occur to anyone that you could be married *and* have a career. It was one or the other. And the further along we got in our careers, the more we realized we did not want to give them up.

The two of us decided, well, we had a mighty nice time living together. After all, we were only two years apart and had always been together anyway. So it was just us two girls until Papa died in 1928 and Mama moved in with us.

After World War Two, we left Harlem

and moved to the Bronx — it was like the country then — so that Mama could have a little cottage with a porch and a garden. We wanted the best for Mama. She was a joy to us.

In 1956, Mama went to Glory and it just about broke our hearts. But she was ninety-five years old, and we had to accept that she had to go sometime. We were so lonesome for her that we moved farther north, to Mt. Vernon. We figured we'd better start over or we'd never get past Mama's leaving us.

That's why we bought this house and have lived in it ever since. It's a quiet spot with a view of New York City and plenty of room for a garden. Yes, it was the perfect spot to retire. Of course, we didn't know we'd be retired *this long!* It's a good thing we found a nice place because we sure have been here awhile.

For about the last thirty-five years, things were mighty quiet. We had a pleasant life, working in the garden, going to church, visiting with friends and neighbors. We took good care of ourselves, doing yoga exercises every morning — except Sunday — and eating carefully. We eat a whole lot of vegetables and fruits and take vitamin supplements.

Then the funniest thing happened: We were discovered! This little gal named Amy Hill Hearth wrote a story about us for *The New York Times*. A book publisher read Amy's article and approached the three of us about doing a book together. Well, we thought we weren't special enough, but Amy convinced us.

We decided to call the book *Having Our Say* because Bessie would keep saying "Well, we're having our say!" as we worked on it. We didn't expect too many people to be interested in it, but it was a best-seller!

Now it seems like the whole world has been writing to us — it seems that a lot of folks, especially young ones, don't know how to live right. We're as old as Moses, so maybe we have learned a few things along the way, and we'd like to pass them on. We hope you find them useful.

— SADIE & BESSIE DELANY
Mt. Vernon, New York
September 1994

1

OLD WAYS, NEW WAYS

WE'RE AS OLD AS THE SKY

Sadie: So you want to live to be 100. Well start with this: No smoking, no drinking, no chewing. And always clean your plate.

Well, you can drink a little bit, but not much!

We get up with the sun, and the first thing we do is exercise. God gave you only one body, so you better be nice to it. Exercise, because if you don't, by the time you're our age, you'll be pushing up daisies.

Most folks think getting older means giving up, not trying anything new. Well, we don't agree with that. As long as you can see each day as a chance for something new to happen, something you never experienced before, you will stay young. Why, we don't feel that we're 105 and 103 — we feel half that old! Even after a century of living, we haven't tried everything. We've only just started.

But when you get to be our age, everyone keeps expecting you to die. That gets mighty annoying! One time a relative made a big fuss because we didn't answer the door. Bessie said, "I guess you thought we were dead. Ha! You'll see! I'll bury *you*." And she was right. We outlived her.

A few years back I had a physical and the nurse asked my birth date. I said 9-19-89. She said, "That's impossible. *This* is eighty-nine." I said, "I meant *eighteen* eighty-nine." Well, she couldn't believe it. She said, "You're one hundred years old! Well, don't tell because no one would ever know."

Just recently, my doctor brought his little boy to meet me. The little boy had the same birthday as me — 9-19-89 — only the little fella was born in *1*989, and I was born in *1*889. The little boy was so excited to meet this lady who was exactly 100 years older than he was!

We never told our age until now. They

say a lady who will tell her age will tell anything else!

THEN AND NOW

People always ask us, "Are things better or worse today?" Well, some things are better and some things are worse. Doctors have more ways to help sick patients today. There's more opportunity for colored folks. But there are a lot of problems in the world today that no one ever dreamed of when we were young. For instance, this business about the environment. Why, clean water was just something you took for granted.

In the old days, another thing you could depend on was the U.S. mail. Why, it was delivered several times a day! And it was faster. If we mailed a letter in New York by midnight, Mama would have it in Raleigh by nine o'clock the next morning.

That's because train service was generally good. Back in the 1890s, Grandma could cook a whole chicken dinner, pack it up, and take it to the train station in Danville, Virginia. It would arrive that same day in Raleigh, still warm, right on time for dinner.

Of course, there are some things that are more convenient today. Washing clothes, for example. When we were children, we didn't even have a well, let alone modern plumbing. So to wash clothes we had to start by going to the spring to get water. Each of us would take three buckets — one for each hand and one for your head. If you wrapped a towel around it for support, you could carry a bucket easily on your head. We'd carry our buckets back to the yard, where we had a great big iron pot and a tub beside it. It took us a few trips to fill them up. Then, using homemade soap, we'd scrub each item of clothing on a washboard. We'd boil the clothes in the pot to clean them, then rinse them in the tub. After rinsing them three times, we'd hang them up to dry. Lord, it was hard work but there's something satisfying about cleaning, as long as you're not in a rush. Doing the wash together, working in that warm, soapy water — it could be soothing, even pleasant.

Now today we have a washer and dryer. But washing machines are very hard on clothes, so we prefer to do most of our wash by hand. Our clothes last forever! We'll use the washboard and then put the clothes in the washer for the rinse cycle. We hardly ever use the dryer. We hang our wash outside on a clothesline or in the basement during the winter. When the sun shines on the clothes, it whitens them. And the fresh air is good for them too.

When we were growing up, we couldn't afford to buy new things, so it was important to take care of what we had. Why, we didn't even have a sewing machine at home back then. When Papa became the first elected Negro bishop of the Episcopal Church in America, Sadie made all his linen vestments herself. It took hours to sew things by hand, but they always looked so nice.

Everything took a lot longer way back when, but you know what? People weren't as frantically busy. Being busy is fine, it's healthy, it's exciting, but folks today just seem to zoom through life! In our day, people had to work hard, so they were tired. They were tired, but they weren't as crazed as folks today.

The two of us at a church bazaar. We haven't stopped having fun just because we're each more than 100 years old. Sometimes we still feel like two schoolgirls.

NEWFANGLED NUISANCES

Bessie: Folks do have some mighty fine gadgets today. For example, there's a gadget that allows you to open the garage door from inside your car. And these small computers that can do anything! Columbia Dental School didn't teach you a thing about bookkeeping, so I sure could have used one of those when *I* was working! And things like sandwich bags and wrapping paper are wonderful; we didn't have anything like that.

Television is an amazing thing. It can educate folks, and it can entertain. But now instead of reading, thinking, or just plain doing, too many folks sit and rot their brains in front of the TV. That's a shame, that folks would take something good and use it badly.

But there are some modern inventions we just plain hate. The worst is the telephone. Of course, when we were younger and I had my dental office, I had to have a phone so patients could reach me. But if you have a phone at home, you give up your privacy and hard-earned peace. Folks are free to bother you whenever they want. And people do all kinds of sneaky things by telephone. Years ago, we knew someone who would call us around five o'clock and say, "I'll be dropping by in an hour or so." Well, she knew we were getting our dinner ready and would feel obliged to set a place for her.

We know that phones can come in handy. We've heard of folks having telephones in their cars, in case they get a flat tire. That seems smart. But it's so much nicer to get a letter. It's permanent. You can read it over and over, thinking about what the person wrote, and when you write back, you have time to figure out what you want to say. But even a letter can't compare to a visit. If you really care about someone, you want to see them, spend a little time together.

Some time ago several of our younger relatives ganged up and forced us to put in a phone. I suppose they were worried about us and wanted to be sure we were all right. They put it right by Sadie's bed. She just hated the sight of that phone — she used to keep it covered with her hat so she wouldn't have to look at it. And the *noise!* Why, it just kept ringing all the time, when we were sleeping or eating or talking to each other, so we refused to answer it. We don't need a phone to talk to each other or to the Lord. What do we need a phone for?

That phone rang so much that I began to fret. "You know, we'd better see what they want," I told Sadie. "Maybe something happened. Maybe somebody's up and died." So she picked it up, and — can you believe it? — it was a collect call. Someone wanted *us* to pay to talk to them!

That was enough for us. We'll never have a telephone again. If that's living in the past, we don't care.

MAKING PEACE WITH THE PAST

Sadie: A lot of folks today are not in touch with the past, and I think that's a shame. Why, upstairs in our house we have a whole wall of family photographs that we've collected over the years. We feel so lucky that we have them. There aren't that many families that can show how they looked more than 100 years ago.

So when our young relatives would come visit, they'd always want to go upstairs to see the pictures, and, of course, we gladly gave them permission. Young people need to know their family history, and it's the responsibility of old folks like us to tell them. Anyway, there was one day that our young nephew came downstairs all upset. He'd just noticed that some of the pictures on the wall were of white men!

"Well," I said, "one of them is your great grandfather James Miliam, and the other is your great-great grandfather Jordan Motley."

But our nephew kept on fussing — about slavery and what happened between white men and colored women and oppression and what-have-you, as if it was news to us. How, he wondered, could we justify giving their pictures a place of honor? It's not that his ideas were entirely wrong, but they started to get Bessie riled up.

She said, "Those people are your ancestors, white or not, and so they're entitled to be up on that wall. You can't pick your relatives — that's the first thing. And the second thing is, those two men left us their land. If they thought enough of their colored relatives to do that, then they're okay by me!"

You can't change the past, and too many folks spend their whole lives trying to fix things that happened before their time. You're better off using your time to improve yourself.

THE COMFORTS OF HOME

Bessie: I'll tell you what I cherish most from the past: our family traditions, all those little rituals that bind you together. Folks today tend to be so busy and independent that they abandon the daily habits, like eating meals together, that keep you close. They think they can watch the TV during dinner or grab a quick bite and rush off. They think it doesn't matter. Well, they are wrong!

When we were growing up, we ate all of our meals together. Supper was the most special time, when we could talk about our day and just enjoy each other's company. It was comforting, and it was fun. Even now that it is just Sadie and me, it's still my favorite time of day. We make it a habit to have supper together — just to sit down at the table and talk. It's not until we're done eating that we bring up serious things, and that's when we make all our big decisions. Or if I want to tell Sadie that something's worrying me — and, honey, there's always something! — that's the perfect time for me to spring it on her.

I'd never give up our suppertimes. Folks who let the little rituals go are missing out on a lot.

FAMILY TIMES

Sadie: The family traditions I love the most are the holiday celebrations. I look forward to the planning, shopping, and cooking almost as much as the holiday itself. You know, you don't need a lot of money to make it special. Why, when we were children, the best Christmas gifts we got would seem cheap today — an orange in each child's stocking. When I think of Christmas, I can still smell those oranges.

For us, Easter Sunday was a holy day, so we'd wait until Easter Monday to have our fun. We'd go out to pick mulberries while Mama hard-boiled the eggs. Then we'd boil up the berries to dye the eggs the nicest shades of pink and red.

On the Fourth of July, Papa would light firecrackers for us. He'd never let us near them because he was afraid we'd get hurt. Funny thing was, he was scared to death of them. Every time he'd light one, he'd toss it and run away like the Devil himself was chasing him. That made us laugh so hard.

Now, birthdays are something else again. We sure have seen a lot of them! Since Bessie and I were both born in September, we've always had a joint celebration. We got in the habit of celebrating on Bessie's birthday — September 3 — because it was easier for Mama. School had already started by the time my birthday arrived on September 19, and Mama was busy. I never minded celebrating my birthday on Bessie's big day. I think it means more to Bessie, anyway.

Bessie starts getting ready the night before. In the morning she gets all dressed up. This is how Bessie got her nickname, "Queen Bess." One year on her birthday, Papa was laughing at her because she was strutting around and he said, "My, my, my. If it isn't Queen Bess herself." And she has to have her favorite cake: a pound cake with fresh coconut icing, served with a Boston cooler — vanilla ice cream in a ginger-ale float. She feels downright sorry for herself if she doesn't have that!

And she won't lift a finger around the house all day. But as she says, "I can't work — I need to spend the day celebrating. That's the least I can do to thank the Lord for another year!"

Bessie: The way we were raised, the first thing you do when you go home — straight from the train station — is visit the family plot. Then you unpack from your trip and see your homefolks. In this picture from the 1960s, I (holding the reins) am with cousin Daisy and her husband, Bigelow, going to pay my respects at Mama's parents' grave seven miles from Danville, Virginia.

2

LESSONS IN LIVING

LOOKING OUT FOR YOURSELF

Sadie: You don't live for a century without picking up a lesson or two. Here's one Bessie taught me: That folks can't take advantage of you if you're doing what you want to.

When we were children, we all had daily chores. Each night, I'd wash the dishes and Bessie would dry, and our little sister Julia would put everything away. Well, Julia was always trying to bribe her way out of work. She'd say, "Bessie, if you put away the dishes, I'll give you a penny." More often than not, Bessie would do it — though she knew very well that Julia didn't have a penny to her name. I would ask Bessie, "How come you fall for that?" And Bessie would say, "Julia's not fooling me one bit. It's just that she hates her job so much and I don't mind it enough to refuse. Now she thinks she owes me a lot and, believe me, I'll get more favors out of her than I could buy with a penny or two!"

I've always been the kind of person who has trouble saying no. During the Depression, everyone needed money, and folks were always coming to us to ask for loans. Well, I made a mistake — I cosigned on a bank loan for a friend who didn't pay it back — and so every week, I let the bank deduct some of my check until I made up every penny. So when people tried to borrow money from me, I had a great excuse. I'd just smile and say, "I'd love to help you out, but you see, my wages are being garnisheed." That sent them packing, and I have to admit that today I still try to find ways to avoid saying just plain no.

If someone asks me a question I don't want to answer, I play dumb. I'll just say, "I don't know" or "I don't remember," though of course I do. It saves fussing, and I just laugh when they go out the door. Why should I care what they think of me?

THE SIMPLE TRUTH

Bessie: I just hate it when Sadie does that, though I have to admit that it works. Now me, I'd rather tell it to you straight! Papa used to say, "Bessie, if I ask you something, I know I'll get the truth." And he was right. I've always found that telling the truth makes life simpler and more comfortable. If you don't, you have to struggle to keep your stories straight, trying to remember what-all you said to which person. I could never stand the strain of that.

Besides, telling a lie is a sign of fear. It means you can't face up to something. Mama always used to say, "If you tell a lie, you must ask yourself what you're afraid of."

I know it can be hard on people to hear the truth. As Sadie says, I can be too blunt. There's a young girl we know who had a baby on her own. I just hate to see a child grow up without a papa, and I can't stand the fact that she threw away her future on account of some no-good man. My opinion hurts her, but try as I might, I just can't hide the way I feel.

I wish I knew another way to tell the truth. You know, it ain't so easy being Bessie!

THE WEB OF LIES

Sadie: Although the truth can hurt, it's dishonesty that can do you greater harm. Here's just one example: When I was a girl, I got walking typhoid fever. Bessie came down with a worse case and had to go into the hospital, but I only had to stay in bed for a few weeks. Well, there was a girl who told everyone that she believed I had gone off to have a baby! She had a bad reputation herself, and so she tried to ruin mine. Can you imagine telling such a lie?

I don't think anyone believed her, but still, that hurt me. My good name means everything to me. As Papa used to say, "Children, all you have in life is your good name. If you lose that, you've got nothing." And it amazed me that the girl wasn't even scared she'd get caught in her lie. That's the thing about dishonest people — they can be very nonchalant about it or even proud of it. They lie to themselves so that they don't feel ashamed. If a person lies about one thing, you can bet, sure as I'm sitting here, that they'll lie about anything.

You might not always like them, but people who are honest are trustworthy. You know they'll keep their word. And as Bessie likes to say, "If you had a roomful of pennies in your house, it wouldn't even occur to you to count 'em when they leave."

THE HARD WAY

Bessie: I have gotten smarter about a few things in my old age, things like taking chances. Now, I know there are folks who are afraid to try anything new, and that's a big problem for them. But me, I was never afraid of anything. I mean, I was always absolutely fearless! Naturally that meant that I didn't always use good sense.

When I was young, we were just getting electricity at Saint Aug's, and Papa warned us not to touch the light fixtures. But I just had to see what all the fuss was about. So I climbed up on a chair and reached for that socket. Next thing I knew, I was glued to it! After a moment, I crashed to the floor. I was lucky I didn't get badly hurt.

Another thing we were told to stay away from was snakes. Of course, we had plenty of snakes in North Carolina, and I knew that many of them were dangerous. But that didn't stop me, no, sir! One day we came across a big old snake and, naturally, I had to go and pick it up. Well, it didn't bite me but it oozed something slimy on my hand and about scared me to death. It was horrible.

I guess I always had to learn things the hard way. I don't know how Mama and Papa put up with it. If there's one lesson I'd like to pass on it's this: Each of us doesn't have to reinvent the world. You don't have to try to do everything yourself. You can learn just as much by watching and listening as by doing.

YOU CAN'T KNOW IT ALL

Sadie: Watching and listening — those are extremely important abilities to develop in yourself. Why, even when I

Papa's favorite picture of Mama, taken about 1885. He carried it in his wallet until the day he died. Our mama was only one-eighth Negro and could have "passed" for white but refused to live a lie. She considered herself to be a Negro, even though her life would have been easier as a white woman.

Papa, around age forty, circa 1898. Some people say a great man is one who is wealthy and powerful, but our measure of a great man is how he treats his wife and children. On our scale, our papa was the greatest.

was teaching, there were plenty of times when my students came up with better ideas than I had. And why shouldn't they? Just because I was the teacher didn't mean that I knew everything. No one can know it all.

Of course, there are lots of folks who act like they know it all. It's a shame, but there are a lot more big talkers in the world than good listeners.

Now, some big talking I like. Take Bessie — that gal could always outtalk anyone you ever met! She'd say, "If you can talk your way into Heaven, I'll surely get there!"

These days, Bessie claims that she doesn't talk so much anymore. She says she's tired of people disagreeing with her opinions. "I used to like a good argument," she says, "but now I don't care about fighting like I used to."

Well, you couldn't prove that by me! If Bessie ever did stop fussing, I'd miss it. I'd be worried to death about her. There are people in this world that God didn't make to keep quiet!

CREATING JOY

Bessie: I'd say one of the most important qualities to have is the ability to create joy in your life. Of course, at my age, it's a joy even to be breathing! Sometimes I joke with Sadie, "I sure am lucky that I'm so good at the things I enjoy the most — eating, sleeping, and talking!"

But when I was younger, I found joy in so many different things. My friends and neighbors. My church. And I dearly loved my flowers and vegetables. We filled our yard with them: wild plum trees, pear trees, fig trees, grapes, blackberries, raspberries, strawberries, African onions, leeks, corn, string beans, okra, squash, cauliflower, cabbage, tomatoes, and rhubarb.

There's nothing like a garden to help you appreciate the passage of time. In the spring, when those brave little crocuses and snowdrops poke up, we cheer them on. Then in March or early April come the daffodils. Then the tulips, and so on, until all the flowers bloom at once: lily of the valley, phlox, black-eyed Susan, cosmos, daisies, and, of course, roses. For some reason, we were always partial to red roses, so we planted more of those.

We never stopped improving our garden. Anytime someone gave us cut flowers as a gift, we would save the seeds and plant them in the spring. Here's a secret: If you're pressed for time, just drop dead flowers on the ground in your garden. The leaves and stems will become mulch and often the seeds will "take" by themselves. There's no need to ever throw out old cut flowers.

The plants I love most are the ones that come from little clippings we brought back years ago from down South. We'd just take a little snip and bring it back and root it. Why, we have a piece of our grandma's rose of Sharon growing right next to our front steps and some of her bridal wreath, too. And we have daylilies and iris lilies from the property of Mrs. Hunter, the wife of the principal at Saint Aug's when we were children. Having those plants is like having our homefolks here with us!

I love my garden so much that I would stay out there all day long if Sadie let me. That's what I mean by creating joy in your life. We all have to do it for ourselves.

Sadie: You know, my life has been filled with joy, too. My joy is Bessie.

To Lead a Good Life

1. Never lose your sense of humor.
The happiest people are the ones who are able
to laugh at themselves.

2. Pay attention to the little things.
One of the best qualities a person can have is
to be observant.
Some people have eyes but they don't see.

3. Think carefully before you promise to do
something. Once you say you'll do it, you'll
have to do it.

4. Know when to keep quiet.
When we decide that something is private,
we'll say it's "graveyard talk." That means it's
between you and me and the tombstone, honey.

5. When somebody is nice to you,
don't take advantage of it.
You don't ride a free horse to death.

6. Put your faith in the Lord, and you'll
never be alone.

3

STANDING ON YOUR OWN

HOW WE DID IT

Sadie: People ask us how we've lived so long, how we got where we did. Well, the key is leading a disciplined life. If you're young, that means working or studying hard. When you're our age, it means exercising every day whether you feel like it or not. A lot of people cringe when they hear the word "discipline." They think it means having no fun. Well, that ain't true, and we're living proof! We have a good time.

Some folks today want to do things the easy way. We have a saying, "They want to get there — without going!" And there isn't any such thing. You've got to pay your dues. You've got to work for it.

Sometimes folks ask us how we put up with racism and sexism to get our advanced college degrees. How could we stand it? Well, what choice did we have? What choice does anyone have? Life's not easy for anyone, despite how it may look. Sometimes you just have to put up with a lot to get the little bit you need.

Now, it's true that you hear of basketball stars and entertainers making it

Dr. Anna J. Cooper at her home in Washington, D.C. All ten of us children were named after somebody. Mama and Papa had no money, and the only way they could honor someone was to name their children after them. Bessie (Annie Elizabeth) was named after Dr. Cooper, who was an educator and early advocate of higher education for colored women.

big with no education. But that's only a tiny, tiny number of people. And it's sad, because a lot of them are too ignorant to know how to live well with their money.

If you are not educated — if you can't write clearly, speak articulately, think logically — you have lost control of your own life.

REACH HIGH!

Bessie: When I was young, I told my papa that I wanted to be a nurse. He said, "Bessie, nursing is a fine profession, but why not try to be a doctor? Reach high!"

Well, I was short a few credits for medical school and I was running out of time, so I became a dentist — only the second colored woman ever licensed to practice in New York State. And I was a good one, I'll tell you! Why, just recently I heard from one of my old dental patients. I did a crown for her back in '29, and you know what? She still had it, more than sixty years later! That makes me so proud.

Pride in a job well done is the one kind of pride God allows you to have. I earned that pride. Nothing brings more satisfaction than doing quality work, than knowing that you've done the very best you can.

Reach high!

DOING FOR YOURSELF

Sadie: Someone asked me recently how I handled students who failed. And I said, "Why, I never failed a student. Not in fifty years of teaching. I worked with the troubled students until they succeeded. I thought that was my job."

Doing quality work — that's what brings you self-respect and that's something folks seem mixed up about today.

Bessie: I used to be known as Dr. Bessie, Harlem's Negro woman dentist. I never worried about catching contagious diseases from my patients because I had faith that God would look after me. I thought, "God didn't give me no gloves."

Sadie: Here I am dressed for horseback riding in North Carolina in the early 1920s. No matter how old you get, you think of yourself as young. In our dreams, we are always young.

You hear all this talk about self-esteem or self-respect, as if it were something other people could give you. But what self-respect really means is knowing that you are a person of value rather than thinking "I am special" in a self-congratulatory way. It means "I have potential. I think enough of myself to believe I can make a contribution to society." It does not mean putting yourself first.

A big part of self-respect is self-reliance — knowing you can take care of yourself. When I started teaching school, I had hardly any money, so I came up with the idea of making candy to sell. Pretty soon, I had a little candy business called Delany's Delights, Inc. My hand-dipped fondant chocolates were sold in shops throughout New York City, including at the Abraham & Straus Department Store, in half-pound, one-pound, and two-pound tins. I charged two dollars a pound, and I made quite a nice little profit! But then the Depression came and I had to shut down my business because no one had the money for luxuries like candy.

Still, that candy kept me going for a long time! It showed me that no matter what happened, I'd never have to be beholden to anyone. Why, I've never needed a handout in my life!

Sadie: My original Delany's Delights candy tin. I didn't wait for a man to come along and take care of me. I made my own money! I had a steady salary from teaching, but I also made good money on my candy business back in the 1920s.

Delany's Delights
SADIE'S HAND-DIPPED FONDANT CHOCOLATES

3 cups sugar
1½ cups water
8 ounces chocolate
(milk or semisweet)

OPTIONAL:
1 teaspoon vanilla extract
or other flavoring

First, make the fondant by boiling the sugar and water in a lightly greased saucepan to the "softball" stage. Pour it into a pan, working it flat with a wide spatula as it cools, until it's creamy.

Next, take a small piece, about the size of the top joint on your little finger, and make it into a small ball. This little piece is then dipped in chocolate (milk chocolate is the most popular) that has been melted in a double boiler ahead of time. The room temperature must be kept cool. (I used to work with my coat on!)

To give the fondant flavor, grind nuts, soften chocolate, grate coconut, or add peppermint flavoring, mixing it into the fondant. Sometimes, you may want to use a flavor that can't be "folded" into the fondant (like whole cherries, pecans, almonds, regular peanuts, brazil nuts). In that case, you dip them, whole, in the fondant, and then in the melted chocolate.

LOOK 'EM IN THE EYE

Bessie: Yes, folks today have got it all wrong. They've got this idea that self-respect means "I am a terrific person. I am wonderful. *Me, me, me.*" That's not self-respect; that's vanity.

But you do need to stand up for yourself. I'm the feisty one. I never took sugar in my tea, no, sir.

The way folks treat you often comes from the way you present yourself. That's why Mama and Papa taught us: "Always look people in the eye." If you don't, they'll think you're afraid of them, that you doubt that you're as good as they are. And then they're all too happy to agree with you!

There's a young boy who helps us with chores who just never could bring himself to look at us. He'd stare at the ground or around the room, mumbling his words, hunching his shoulders. So Sadie and I decided to make him our little project. We started telling him, "Stand up straight. Speak clearly — don't swallow those words." And especially, of course, we'd say to him, "Look me directly in the eye."

It took awhile to break him of his habits, but the change in him was amazing. His voice got louder. His enunciation improved. His confidence grew. He even seemed taller!

You won't believe what finally happened. One day he came over and, standing proud and tall, he looked Sadie straight in the eye. And in a clear, strong voice, he offered her a deal. "For a dollar, I'll feed your dog every day. But all I'll do is feed him. I'm not washing out his dish."

Well, that sure made us laugh! Some folks might say we taught him a lesson that he learned a little too well, but we were kind of proud of him. We hope he carries that spirit with him for the rest of his life!

4

LEANIN' ON THE LORD

THE SPIRIT WORLD

Sadie: For us there was never a time when we did not believe in God. There's a lot in this world you can't see that you still believe in, like love and courage. Well, that's the way it is with faith. Just because you can't hold it in your hand doesn't mean it's not there. A person who has faith is prepared for life and to do something with it.

When we were growing up, Papa kept the Bible in his study, and we'd get a reading from it every night before we went to sleep. Papa always handled the Bible very carefully. He used to tell us never to put anything on top of it, not even a piece of paper. It was sacred.

That Bible — the Word of God — was the center of our home, and you know, we still have it. We keep it in the living room, on a special small table between the two chairs where we spend most of our time.

The Bible is where we go for guidance. God's wisdom is at work in the words, but you can also get plenty of practical advice in the Bible. After all, mankind hasn't changed that much.

We find a lot of comfort in the old prayers and hymns, too. Why, one of the greatest gifts we've received in recent years was a copy of the old Cokesbury hymnal. It's a Methodist hymnal filled with songs we hadn't heard in nearly 100 years. Our papa was an Episcopal bishop, but his family had been Methodists. So when he got lonesome for his people, he used to play those old Methodist hymns on the piano.

Such beautiful songs, those old hymns, and the old spirituals too. With all the years of tradition behind them, they're bound to lighten your heart. Here's one that Bessie loves to sing:

> *What kind of shoes*
> *Are you going to wear*
> *Golden slippers*

What kind of shoes
Are you going to wear
Golden slippers
Golden slippers, I'm going to wear
Golden slippers, I'm going to wear
When I go up to live
With my Lord
Going up
Going up
Going up
I'm going up to live
With my Lord

Those old songs helped the Negro slaves, like our papa, survive; they kept them going. Those songs keep the Spirit in our lives.

PRAISING THE LORD

Bessie: When we walk into our house — whether we're coming back from a long trip or just from seeing the neighbors — the first thing we say is, "We're home. Praise the Lord." We do that to honor Him, to thank Him for watching over us.

Of course, there are times when I wish the Lord *wasn't* watching, like when I run my mouth or lose my temper. I try to do right; I try not to stray. As Sadie says, "If you want to climb that ladder to Heaven, you've got to treat every day as if it's Judgment Day."

I think God understands that I'm only human. He gave me this mouth, He gave me a temper, and so I'm bound to err. I'm sure I must be getting credit for trying! But every once in a while, just to keep on His path, I try to take in an old-fashioned fire-and-brimstone sermon. I'm an Episcopalian, and I appreciate the thoughtful preaching in my Church — but there's nothing like fire and brimstone to set me straight.

Fight fire with fire, I always say!

SWEET HOUR OF PRAYER

Sadie: We set aside some time every day to talk to the Lord. We got that habit from Mama. She had a full-time job running the school, plus ten children to raise, but there was never a day in her life that she didn't reserve one full hour to pray. She had a beautiful writing desk where she kept her special things, like her own Bible and prayer book. Above it were two pictures of her heroes — Abraham Lincoln and Frederick Douglass — and when she sat down between them, we knew we had to leave her alone. That was her hour with the Lord.

Today we have Mama's writing desk in our living room and I keep those two pictures over my bed. They remind us that no one is ever too busy or pressured or tired to make a time and place for God in their lives. After all, He has to manage the whole world, and He's never too busy for us!

THE LORD'S WAYS

Bessie: I'm always amazed at the power of prayer. You know, I've always had trouble putting out of my mind and forgiving some of the mean people I've encountered in my life — you know the bigots we used to call rebby boys. Then somebody suggested, "Pray for each and every one of them. Put them at the *top* of your prayer list." Well, I didn't like that idea at all. I said, "*What!* You expect *me* to pray for those nasty old rebby boys?" But recently I tried it. I just about choked on the words. But, Lord, it did make me feel better.

Sometimes I don't understand the Lord's ways, but who am I to question? I'm just a person, and I don't know why.

WE'RE IN HIS HANDS

You never know when or how the Lord will take a hand in your life. Here's an example: In *Having Our Say*, we told about Papa's being invited, back in 1918, to give a guest sermon at Christ Church in Raleigh. The invitation was a great honor, and so our whole family came to attend the service. But when we got to the church, they stuck us way on up in the balcony because we were colored. They made us sit where the *slaves* had been made to sit. And then we were not given the privilege of Communion.

Well, after our book came out, you won't believe what we got in the mail. A formal letter of apology from the congregation of that church! We were so touched that they apologized a full seventy-five years later.

Now, *that's* God's work.

5

THEY DON'T HAVE POCKETS IN HEAVEN

SAVING AND SPENDING

Bessie: Money is the root of every mess you can think of. There's some folks who would kill you for a nickel. Those are the sorriest folks of all.

Anyone who lives for money is surely missing the best things in life. There's satisfaction in doing, in helping. There's an old saying, "Money is useful, but don't let it use you."

Papa was terrible with money; he was *too* generous. If someone in the neighborhood back home couldn't pay his rent, he knew that Papa would give him the money. Finally, Mama had to take charge.

When people began to find out they couldn't get Papa's money anymore, they got mad. We had a cousin who said, "Your papa is so cheap that if the Statue of Liberty was shimmying, he wouldn't pay a nickel to see it."

I guess I inherited some of Papa's habits. Why, the whole time I was a dentist, I never raised my rates. So I'm always surprised today by what folks charge. A few years back we had a lawyer who charged a $150 an hour! Well, she came to our house and was carrying on about our garden and this and that. I cut her off. "Excuse me," I said, "but if you're charging a hundred fifty dollars an hour I can't pay you to chit-chat!" After our book came out, that lawyer asked if she could come by to visit with a friend. "Well," I said to Sadie, "if we let her, I suppose we should charge *her* a hundred fifty dollars an hour! Ha-ha!" We didn't charge her, of course.

I never had to charge my patients much because we always lived so cheaply. One time, Sadie read in a magazine about a woman who had figured out a way to cook dinner for her family for a $1.50 per person. And she said, "Bessie, I can surely beat that!" And sure enough, she did it for 75 cents per person. The trick is, you must cook from scratch, and you must shop wisely. For instance, we always buy what's on special. And once we're home, we store the food carefully so we never waste it.

Maybe because we were raised to practice thrift, we don't want to be rich! They say it's easier for a camel to pass through the eye of a needle than for a rich man to get into Heaven. We know the only thing money can buy that you really need is food on the table and a roof over your head.

Think about this: When I was a young woman, I went by boat on a trip to Jamaica. It was such a beautiful place! The sun, the flowers, the blue water. Everyone took it slow, enjoyed themselves. They knew how to live well! But you know what? So many of those folks wanted to come to New York. That was their dream. They wanted money.

All I could say was, "Don't you realize that you already have what money can't buy?" They had it in the palm of their hands and didn't even know it.

I'll tell you a story: Not long ago we went into New York City to be guests on a TV show. Well, those folks sent a limousine to pick us up. It was the biggest automobile we ever laid our eyes on. It was called a "stretch" limousine. We climbed in and sat way back at the end — and I just had to laugh. I told Sadie, "We could *live* out of this car!"

That was a joke, but it told the truth. People who care about things like limousines are courting trouble.

MAKING THE MOST OF THINGS

Sadie: We recently had to start recycling our garbage where we live. Since we never have much garbage, it wasn't a big problem for us. Any leftovers we have we give to our dog, and we reuse things anyway. For instance, if we use paper towels to clean up spilled water, we lay them out to dry and reuse them. We don't throw them out. We never waste a thing — not even things like corn cobs or watermelon rind. We use them to make wine or the best pickles you ever tasted.

Watermelon Rind Pickles

Rinds from 1 watermelon
2¼ cups sugar
¾ cup water

PICKLING SPICES:
1 teaspoon mixed (pickling) spices
2 sticks cinnamon
½ teaspoon cinnamon
½ teaspoon allspice
1 lemon, sliced
¾ cup vinegar

First, soak the rinds in salt water. After a few hours, peel the rinds. Then soak the rinds overnight in fresh water, in the icebox, in a covered pot.

The next morning, scald the rinds in boiling water for a few minutes, then cool them thoroughly. Put them in the icebox overnight again, covered with fresh water.

For 1 quart of pickles, heat up ¾ cup of sugar to dissolve in ¾ cup of water with the pickling spices. Pour over the rinds in a quart jar and let stand.

The following day, add ½ cup of sugar and ½ cup of vinegar. Bring to a boil, then remove from the heat. The next day, add ½ cup of sugar and ¼ cup of vinegar.

On the last day, add ½ cup of sugar. Simmer until the rinds are clear. Pack them into clean, hot quart jars. Fill with the pickling syrup to within ½ inch of the tops. Process for 10 minutes in a boiling water bath canner, according to the manufacturer's instructions.

Corn Cob Wine

1 dozen raw corn cobs
1 gallon boiling water
2 packages yeast
9 cups sugar

Place cobs in a container and pour boiling water over them. Cover *loosely* with cheesecloth or a dish towel and let stand for 24 hours. Remove the cobs and add the yeast and sugar. Cover loosely again and let stand for 9 days. Strain through cheesecloth, cover loosely, and store in a moderately cool place until it is fermented, which may take as long as 10 weeks.

DON'T SCRIMP ON MAMA

Bessie: Now, there are a few things that are worth spending money on. For instance, when Mama was in her nineties, she needed special orthopedic shoes. Well, the man at the shoe store kept acting like Sadie and I were foolish to want to buy the *best* shoes for Mama. What he meant was, Why spend that kind of money on someone so old, someone who's going to die any day? Well, that made me furious! So we went and bought Mama the best pair, just like we had planned. We didn't have much, but giving Mama the things she needed — that was never a waste of money.

How to Handle Money

1. When it comes to money, keep your mouth shut.

2. Cut back on your possessions. The more you own, the more time you waste taking care of things.

3. Don't spend what you don't have. Forget credit cards — they are the Devil's work!

4. Don't live above your income. If your income goes down, your spending must go down.

5. Out of every dollar, give the first ten cents to the Lord, the second ten cents to the bank for hard times, and keep the rest — but you'd better spend it wisely.

6. Once you put your hard-earned money in the bank, leave it there! Smart people invest it, and then they'll always have some to fool with.

7. Teach your children to save money from day one. Give your child an allowance so she can practice responsibility. A child who doesn't learn thrift at home will have money trouble all her life.

THE REAL THING

Sadie: Living cheaply isn't a burden to us at all. It takes a little more time, but there are some things — like store-bought soap — that cost a lot and just aren't as good as homemade. Why, I've never bought a bar of soap in my life! I made my own, and we use it in the bath, for the laundry, and even to wash our teeth! Even my neighbors swear by my soap. There was a little girl with sensitive skin, and her mother said my soap was the only kind that made her feel better.

If you make soap, here's something you have to watch out for. The last time I made it, I put it outside in the sun on our porch and Bessie noticed this neighborhood tom cat hanging around. She said, "Sadie, that old cat is sniffing around your soap!" I was afraid maybe he'd do something nasty to that soap, after we'd about killed ourselves making it. Don't worry; we ran him off.

Sadie's Soap

Some of these ingredients, such as lye, are poisonous, so be very careful handling them. Be sure to keep small children out of the kitchen!

6 pounds grease, melted and clean (or three pounds grease and 3 pounds olive, coconut, or other rich oil)
1 cup borax
½ cup water, boiled
2 tablespoons sugar
1 tablespoon washing soda
1 cup sudsy ammonia
1 can (13 ounces) pure lye
2 pints plain water

OPTIONAL:
2 ounces glycerin
2 to 4 tablespoons perfume, such as oil of cloves
2 cups oatmeal

Start by dissolving the lye in the 2 pints of water in a porcelain container. Set aside and allow to cool until the mixture is just warm. This may take a few hours.

Collect grease from cooking until you have about 6 pounds (or render it from fat bought from a butcher). Make sure you drain it through cheesecloth so that you remove any little pieces of meat. (Half solid fat and half liquid fat makes the best soap.)

Next, put the borax in a porcelain pan. Add the ½ cup of boiled water and the sugar and washing soda.

Next, add the sudsy ammonia. Follow at once with the lye and 2 pints of water, checking first to see that the lye water is just slightly warm. Hold your hand over it — don't stick a finger in it. Then add the melted grease, a third at a time. Stir constantly until it's the consistency of thick cream. (Both grease and the lye solution need to be lukewarm to make good soap.)

If you're making facial soap, when the mixture is thick as honey, add the glycerin and perfume. Sometimes we add 2 cups of oatmeal run through a food chopper to give the soap texture.

When you're done, put the soap into paper boxes lined with freezer paper. When it gets thick, cut it into bars. Then put it in the sun until it bleaches white. Store for use.

One nice feature of this soap is that it floats!

Sometimes the old ways are still the best ways. You can't get clothes cleaner than with a washboard, and nothing beats homemade soap.

6

FIRST THINGS FIRST

IF IT HELPS JUST ONE PERSON

Just about every problem you can think of in this world could be solved in the home if folks were brought up right. There is nothing more important than having a good mama and papa, loving but strict. There were ten children in our family, but our parents were never too busy to reach out to the world. In fact, our family motto was "Your job is to help someone." Mama always said, "If it helps just one person, it's worth doing."

There was a student at Saint Aug's when we were growing up who was so homesick she would sit and cry. Her name was Josephine. Well, Josephine just wanted to give up and go home to her people. Finally, Mama said, "Why don't you come live with us?" And she came to live with our family and she finished school. And you know, she never left our family. She got a job working as a nanny for our brother Lemuel, who was a doctor.

That was the example that Mama and Papa set for us, and we've tried to follow it all of our lives. And you know what else they taught us? That color shouldn't matter. Why, when we were children, there was a white missionary at Saint Aug's who had a tiny baby with severe diaper rash. The woman didn't know how to take care of it. Mama told her, "I know how to fix that rash." So she took the child, bathed and powdered him, and in a few days he was fine. Mama took care of that white baby as if he were her own.

One time, when Bessie was studying dentistry at Columbia, she was with some colored friends and they encountered a drunken man who had collapsed in the subway. She stopped to help the man, and they said, "Why are you bothering with him? He's white." She said, "Can't you see he needs help?"

We don't see folks as black or white.

This race mess is just plain foolishness! And the fighting that goes on between religions is crazy, too. Papa used to get very upset when he'd hear anti-Semitic remarks. He wouldn't stand for it. He'd say, "The Jews are God's Chosen People. Who are you, who couldn't make a flea, to disrespect God by criticizing the Jews?"

The world is full of nice folks, whatever their color or religion. As Mama used to say, your job is to find them.

THE RIGHT TRAINING

Sadie: I can't get over the litter on the ground in New York City. People eat a sandwich, they throw the wrapper on the ground. You might think that's a little thing to be provoked about, but it's not a little thing. It shows a lot about the character of the person, that he doesn't care about anyone else. It's plain bad manners!

We hate bad manners. By "manners" I don't mean using the right fork or spoon at the dinner table. All I'm talking about is performing simple acts of consideration, which sounds easy — and it is easy, but too few people even bother to try.

Here's an example: One day a friend was visiting us, a woman. While we were talking the doorbell rang, and our friend got up to let the person in. It was a man who lived nearby and — would you believe it? — he just charged right in and grabbed her chair. Just sat right down, leaving her standing there. Anyone could see that there was nowhere else for her to sit. He didn't even notice!

By the time he got up and left, Bessie was just steaming. She said, "Can you imagine someone being so rude?" But I had to point out — and she agreed — that it wasn't all his fault. He had what we call "poor training."

His parents are to blame for not teaching him the basic rule of courtesy — to be aware when you've inconvenienced someone else. If you get that lesson early, being thoughtful is a habit, something you do automatically. It's almost impossible for adults to learn that later on.

Our family in 1901. We're standing in the back row. Growing up, we had no money at all, but we had good parents, plenty of love, and a roof over our heads. One of the greatest joys in life is having a blessed childhood, and we have carried that with us all these years.

'FESSING UP

Bessie: One of the great gifts my parents gave me was a conscience, a real sense of right and wrong. That's not something you're born with. You develop it by watching adults, of course, but even more, you have to work at it.

Here's how we did it: Every night before we went to bed, Papa would tell us to be quiet and to reflect on our deeds of the day. Then he'd ask us, one by one, to confess all the naughty things we'd done that day. That's the first step — to be willing to admit your mistakes.

The next step is to ask the Lord's forgiveness for each error. Acknowledging them helps make sure you learn from them. And it keeps you from skipping over some!

The last step is still the hardest for

me. I always say, "Forgiving is nothing compared to forgetting." It's bad enough to tell your failings to the Lord, but to apologize — I never *could* stand that! The worst was when Papa made us kiss and make up with our brothers and sisters. And to avoid it, why, I just had to be good!

You know, I'll bet that's why Papa made me do it!

Sadie: I am third from the right in this picture of my graduating class at Saint Augustine's School, 1910. When you get an education, you don't just help yourself; you lift up everyone around you. And here's my diploma from Columbia University, 1920.

THE·TRUSTEES·OF·COLUMBIA·UNIVERSITY
IN·THE·CITY·OF·NEW·YORK
TO·ALL·PERSONS·TO·WHOM·THESE·PRESENTS·MAY·COME·GREETING
BE·IT·KNOWN·THAT
SARAH·LOUISE·DELANY
HAVING·COMPLETED·THE·STUDIES·AND·SATISFIED·THE·REQUIREMENTS
FOR·THE·DEGREE·OF
BACHELOR · OF · SCIENCE
HAS·ACCORDINGLY·BEEN·ADMITTED·TO·THAT·DEGREE·WITH·ALL·THE
RIGHTS·PRIVILEGES·AND·IMMUNITIES·THEREUNTO·APPERTAINING
IN·WITNESS·WHEREOF·WE·HAVE·CAUSED·THIS·DIPLOMA·TO·BE
SIGNED·BY·THE·PRESIDENT·OF·THE·UNIVERSITY·AND·BY·THE·DEAN·OF
TEACHERS·COLLEGE·AND·OUR·CORPORATE·SEAL·TO·BE·HERETO·AFFIXED
IN·THE·CITY·OF·NEW·YORK·ON·THE · TWENTY-FIFTH · DAY·OF·FEBRUARY
IN · THE · YEAR · OF · OUR · LORD · ONE · THOUSAND · NINE · HUNDRED · AND
TWENTY

DEAN

PRESIDENT

CROWLEY, JAMES A.   *Psi Omega*

Hoboken High School; Wm. Carr Dental Society.

Another member of the gang.
Ah, Jimmy dear, your dome shines bold
But all that glitters is not gold.

DELANEY, ANNIE E.   *Delta Sigma*

St. Augustine's School.

Way down deep
In one of the warm
Remote corners of all our hearts
We shall carry with us
Into the prosaic practical
World of Dentistry,
The memory of
A perfect lady,
Bessie Delaney.

1923

Bessie: Here are my yearbook picture and diploma from Columbia School of Dental and Oral Surgery, 1923. I was the only Negro woman in my dental school class, and I was mighty lonely, but I didn't let that stop me. I wanted to be the best dentist that ever lived. People said, "But she's a woman; she's colored," and I said, "Ha! Just you wait and see."

College of Dental and Oral Surgery of N. Y.

302-6 East 35th Street

New York   **June 1, 1923**

Miss Annie E. Delaney

Dear Madam:—

         You are herewith notified that your work for the Senior ..... year has been .... satisfactory and has been accepted .... by the Faculty.

Yours truly,

Worthington Russell

SECRETARY OF THE FACULTY.

Our family on a rooftop in Harlem during the 1920s. A measure of a close family is how much the children stay in touch when they're grown. There were ten of us, and all but one moved to Harlem after World War One. They used to say about us Delanys: "You never see <u>one</u>. Where there's one, there's <u>two</u>."

WHEN IT COMES TO CHILDREN

Between caring for our brothers and sisters and all the children we've helped over the years, we feel like we've raised the whole world!

Sadie: I was always a softie when it came to children. I found out early that if I was kind, they would do anything for me. But being kind doesn't mean being permissive. Children need to learn discipline and responsibility. People used to ask Mama, "Why is it that your girls never seem to be in any trouble?" And Mama used to say, "I keep them *busy.*"

If you live right, chances are your children will, too. But teach them *everything.* What you don't teach them, someone else will — and you may not like those lessons!

Bessie: What children need most is love and attention. That doesn't mean spoiling them or letting them boss you. That doesn't mean letting them do what *they* want to do. But just sit with them, listen to them, look at them. A lot of people don't even *look* at their children.

The most important thing is to teach your child compassion. A complete human being is one who can put himself in another's shoes.

A WORD ON BITTERNESS

Negro parents should be careful not to fill their children's hearts with anger. If your child runs into prejudice, just tell 'em, "The world can be a mighty mean place sometimes." And give 'em a big hug and just go on.

It's understandable that colored folks are bitter. The only problem is, their bitterness won't change a thing. It will ruin *their* lives. If we'd been bitter and full of hate, we'd never have lived the pleasant life we've lived. Sometimes we get mad, but there's a big difference between anger and bitterness.

As Papa used to say, "They can segregate you but they can't control your mind. Your mind's still yours, no matter what they do."

WASTING A WORRY

People who intermarry tend to worry a lot about their children. They're afraid their children will have to choose between the races, that they'll have what they call an "identity crisis."

Well, we're part white and part Negro — our mama was mostly white — but we don't have any identity crisis. We're just ourselves, that's all! We're proud of who we are. We think of ourselves as colored people.

So we don't see anything wrong with interracial relationships. If two people can find happiness in this world, who cares what color they are?

Our advice to parents raising children of mixed race: Don't let your children get the idea from you that it's a problem. Our parents didn't fret about it, at least in front of us. Maybe that's why we don't worry about it, either.

A Word to Young People

1. Don't have babies before you're ready — and "ready" means being married! Raising children is the hardest work you'll ever do. It's selfish to deny a child its best chances in life, and it's foolish to deny yourself a future.

2. Finish school. A diploma may seem just a piece of paper, but it's worth a whole lot more than any paper money in the whole world. No matter what happens in your life — if you lose your savings, if you lose your home — an education will let you start over. It is the one thing that no one can ever take away from you.

3. Don't fool with drugs or folks who do drugs! They have nothing to offer you but trouble.

4. Don't be afraid to fail. Even if you do, you're bound to learn something along the way.

7

HOMEFOLKS

WELCOMING FRIENDS

Sadie: Homefolks. What are homefolks? The most important people in the world: your neighbors and kin back home. Or perhaps a very, very special person who is new in your life. It's a great compliment to say "So-and-so is just like homefolks!"

When we find homefolks, we sure appreciate them. We've always had a lot of friends, many going back to our Saint Aug's days. Some of those friendships lasted longer than most people stay alive. One of our special friends was named Elizabeth Gooch, or "Gooch," as we called her. She was a maiden lady who lived with her sister, just like we do. Well, when Gooch's sister died, Bessie said, "We'd better take the train and get on down there to Covington, Kentucky, to see how old Gooch is doing."

So we packed our bags and went on out. Gooch seemed to be doing fine, but if she hadn't been okay, we would have brought her back to New York to live with us. That's the sort of thing homefolks do for one another.

For true happiness, you've got to have companionship — other people, preferably one key person — in your life. It doesn't have to be a husband or a wife. It can be a friend or, like us, a sister. You can confide in a sister, share your secrets, and talk over your troubles with her. If you have a fuss, you have to make up. With a sister, you know it's forever. We always say that we've never had one best friend except each other.

By now, we've outlived just about everyone we used to know, so many of our new friends are much younger than we are. That doesn't matter as long as you care about the same things and, just as important, if you have the same sense of humor. And you know what? Younger people can teach you a lot. They keep you up to date. So we'll take homefolks wherever we find them!

One day, we were talking about our age and how soon we expect to go to Glory, and it made one of our young friends sad. She said, "I sure am going to miss you two someday." Well, Bessie told her, "Don't you worry, child. If anyone messes with you, I'll just put the curse on them from the Spirit World!"

Yes, we know how to look out for our friends!

GOOD AS GOLD

Bessie: When we talk about looking out for our friends, we're talking about loyalty. That's one of the most admirable qualities in a person and — yes, sir! — it's one of the rarest. I have to say that we've been mighty lucky in finding special, loyal friends. Take our friend Lulu. She came from Saint Simons Island, Georgia, and she was a nurse. Whenever there was trouble in our family, like when Mama took sick, Lulu would come to visit and help us out. We never even had to ask.

Lulu died recently, and her niece sent us two beautiful afghans that Lulu had just finished crocheting. The niece wrote, "I don't think anyone in the world would enjoy these more than you two." She was right!

If you find friends like Lulu — folks you can trust and count on to show up when you need them most — hang on to 'em. You've struck gold!

COMPANY IS KING!

Sadie: There's nothing more rewarding than welcoming friends into your home. We always use the back door in our house, and that's where folks we see a lot, like neighbors, come in, too. We keep the front door only for our guests. It's to honor them — to show them that they're special. When company comes, we drop whatever we're doing. Company is king for us!

We've always had friends and family coming by, more than we could handle. That's a compliment! Why, there was a time when we made four cakes every week to serve company. Two we varied, but one was always chocolate and the other was always a pound cake. Here's how we made it.

Sadie's Pound Cake

1 cup butter
½ cup shortening (e.g., Crisco)
2½ cups sugar
4 cups flour (3 cups cake flour, unsifted;
   1 cup all purpose)
1 teaspoon salt
½ teaspoon baking powder
1 teaspoon mace
⅔ cup milk
1 tablespoon vanilla extract
1 teaspoon lemon extract
1 teaspoon almond extract
6 eggs
¼ cup vegetable oil

An hour or so ahead of time, take all of the ingredients out of the icebox so that they are room temperature when you start. Put all of them in a mixing bowl except the eggs and oil. Beat by hand, or low speed on a mixer, for 5 minutes. Next, beating at medium speed, add the eggs, one at a time. Then add the oil and beat for 5 more minutes. Pour into a greased pan and bake at 325 degrees for 40 minutes. Then turn up the heat to 350 degrees and bake about 20 minutes more, or until the top springs back when you touch it.

BEST FRIENDS

Bessie: You know, animals are some of the best companions you can have. One of my best friends is my little dog. He's a stray, he's no good, but I love him. I feed him part of my dinner every night. He always gets the best part, and I feed him *first*. But my little dog can be a lot of trouble. Why, one time I locked him in the basement because he was naughty, and you know what that rascal did? He chewed all the leather buttons off my best dress that I had hanging in the basement on my clothesline. And I said to him, "Those folks who owned you before, they were going to get rid of you. Maybe they had the right idea!"

But I didn't really mean that. I just had to give him a piece of my mind.

Sadie: Bessie's at war with that little dog. He bedevils her. When he hides, he won't come out when Bessie calls to him. I say, "Bessie, don't you realize? He won't come because he knows you'll punish him." So I call and he comes right out and hides behind me. That just makes Bessie furious!

But she always forgives him. Those two just love each other. Sometimes I think Bessie loves animals as much as she loves people!

THE TIES THAT BIND

Sadie: You know, it's the simplest things that form the strongest ties between people — like shared memories, even silly ones. For instance, when we were children we had as a pet a black kitty with a long black tail that stood straight up. Bessie just loved to play with that cat but he'd always try to get away. One time when the cat was escaping with

Bessie chasing after him, she called out to me, "Catch him, Sadie! Catch him by the *handle!*"

Another time, when Bessie was still in a high chair, Mama was feeding her while talking to somebody. Without really watching, she just kept putting spoonful after spoonful of food into Bessie's mouth. Bessie started getting flustered — she hates to be ignored — and I guess she'd had enough to eat. So she started saying, "Plenty, Mama! Plenty!" We still laugh about that.

These things happened over 100 years ago, but I still like to tease Bessie about them. You know the older you get, it's the funny little things that bring you the most pleasure. You like to recall them over and over again. Those are the stories that make a family or a friendship, and I cherish them.

GETTING INVOLVED

Bessie: Some people, older people especially, tend to draw into themselves. They're afraid of getting to know their neighbors or they're not interested. They grow isolated. That's a big mistake! You never know when you might need other people, but you need to earn their help. You have to contribute to your community.

Papa taught us that. He was so thoughtful that even if it was cheaper to go someplace else, he shopped locally. Even in the days when a few cents made a big difference, supporting our neighbors was more important than the money.

The Bible says you should love *all* your neighbors. Sometimes that's not easy! The worst are folks who are nosy but don't share a thing about themselves. We had a woman like that living near us once. She'd come right out and ask you anything, put you on the spot, and store up opinions about you. Sadie just stayed away from her, but she drove me wild. Of course, I can be a little nosy and opinionated, too!

A little nosiness can be a good thing. We've been retired a long time, so we're home all day, and our neighbors are glad to have us keeping an eye on the street. Like if we notice strange cars or people who don't belong in someone's yard — chances are they're up to no good. We belong to what they call a "neighborhood watch," and if we see something fishy, we go for help.

Some working parents nearby don't want their kids home alone after school. Who can blame them? So we help out by having the children stop off with us. One child would do her homework on our dining-room table until her folks got home, and one day she got stuck on her arithmetic. So I said, "Bring it over here. Maybe I can help you." Why, that child was so surprised. She just couldn't imagine that two old ladies like us could know arithmetic! Well, we showed her what to do, and the lesson she got that day was a lot more valuable than arithmetic. She learned to be more open-minded about people, not to assume, not to judge.

So we do our little bit. Getting involved is satisfying. It keeps us busy and makes us useful. Everyone has something to contribute!

8

A HEAP OF TROUBLE

MEN AND WOMEN

Bessie: Today, sex is everywhere, all over the newspapers and the TV. Kids hear all about it, and so they get interested in it early. They know it's something grown-up, so they want to try it. They get the idea it's the most important thing in life.

In our day, it was different. Everything about sex was deeply private. Why, even with as many brothers as we had, boys were a mystery to us. Our parents kept us apart — the girls had their own room and the boys had theirs. Your little cot was all you had in the world that was truly yours. No one else slept in it, or even sat on it during the day.

I remember one time, when I was eight or nine years old, I asked Mama if my little brother Nap could sleep with me. We planned to get up before dawn and go pick "cressie greens," or wild watercress. But even though we'd wake up half the family with us, Mama said no. It just wasn't proper.

When we got older, of course, we had our share of beaux. We didn't want to marry because we'd have to give up our careers — and we'd worked too hard to do that! One man who wanted me to marry him was Dean, a dentist from Brooklyn whose family had a house in Sag Harbor. He finally gave up, saying, "I guess it's just as well. Folks in your family live a long time while mine tend to die young. You could be a widow forever." And you know, he was right. Dean died when he was only forty-six years old.

And there was a physician from Philadelphia, Dr. MacDougald, who really wanted to marry Sadie. His first wife had died and he had a young daughter, who still keeps in touch with Sadie to this day. But marriage proposals or no marriage proposals, we always respected ourselves enough to act like ladies. In return, those men treated us with the utmost decency. A lot in this world has changed, but men haven't changed that much. Women would get along a lot better today if they maintained their self-respect and decency.

I'll tell you a funny story about decency. Not long ago, I pulled a muscle in my back while exercising, and when the word got out, one of our neighbors — a man — came over to offer me a *massage*. That's right! He wanted to rub my whole body, from my neck to my backside. I was speechless for once in my life. All I could say was, "Oh, no thanks!" After he left, Sadie and I broke out laughing, and I said, "That man is crazy! Ain't no man gonna rub Bessie Delany's back! I never let 'em do that when I was young, and I'm surely not about to start now, no, sir."

FUSSIN' WITH FELLAS

Sadie: We had six brothers, so believe

me, we know a lot about men. Men always want you fretting over them. One time one of our brothers moved in with us. His wife had died and we felt sorry to see him, all alone, so we took him in. Bessie gave up her room and he filled it with his stuff — man-type things like guns and other junk. That was hard enough, but he drove us crazy when he started getting bossy. He'd complain, "Chicken for dinner *again?*" We were so relieved when he remarried and moved out. We'd had just about enough of him.

But there are worse things that women have to watch out for. There are a lot of men who are out for only two things: intimacy and money. When our papa was dying back in 1928, Bessie had to rush back to Raleigh from Harlem by train. She was just closing the door to her office when this man, a friend of hers, showed up and asked for money. She said, "The only money I got in this world I need to go see my papa on his deathbed." Do you know what that rascal said? He said, "You must have more money than that. You work like a dog, you don't go out much, and you don't even dress well." Now she says she wonders why she didn't pop that old fella in the mouth. Who did he think he was?

We were good-looking gals and it always got us in trouble. Men are a heap of trouble, just a heap of trouble. But we don't want to say that men are always in the wrong. Women aren't perfect, either. A lot of them look for the wrong kind of men — good-lookin' dudes, men with money, smooth-talking operators. It takes a smart woman to fall for a good man!

There are not too many men in the world like our papa. In our home, Papa was the head of the household, but he always treated Mama with great respect. Papa and Mama had a lifelong love affair, the way it ought to be.

WHAT ARE THOSE
GALS THINKING?

Bessie: I'll tell you something: Women don't know how to put themselves together today. Especially those hairdos — I don't think too much of them. It's like gals look in the mirror and say, "Hmmmm, let's see just how ugly I can make myself look today." That goes for the white gals as well as the colored.

I really dislike that hairdo called "dreads." We had a young relative come to visit us who'd done her hair in dreads and she asked us what we thought. Sadie was polite. She said, "Well, you know I liked the way you used to do your hair a little better." But I told her the truth: "It looks terrible! God didn't make you ugly enough, now you've gone and improved on the situation!"

Women today aren't modest. In our

day, women tried to dress well, in clothes with good fabrics and flattering lines. But now you'll see these gals in tight pants and short skirts — they show everything! And it seems like the bigger the butt, the shorter the skirt! What are those gals thinking? Then they say that men don't treat 'em right or that no one takes them seriously on the job!

Mercy! Those gals are crazy. In our day you could get in enough trouble with just the ankle showing, yes, sir!

THE RIGHT HUSBAND

Sadie: A lot has changed for women today. It used to be that women were very secretive about their pregnancies. Mama used to wear these big long dresses that covered up practically everything. You could hardly tell she was pregnant until the baby was just about born. So recently we were surprised when we had a journalist visit who was very, very pregnant. Bessie whispered, "I think she's going to drop that baby! In our house! We better boil some water!"

We had no idea that women nowadays worked right up until their time. I guess we learned something new.

Of course, when we were young, it was rare for married women to work at all. But today, it's common, even for those with children. There's no reason that mothers can't also have careers. But to do that, you need to have the right husband.

A man who's too selfish to look after his own children, who won't give them his time, well, that's the wrong husband. That man is no better than an overgrown child himself. How can he call himself a papa?

Every child needs a papa when he's growing up. Why, we'd be nothing without our papa!

WOMAN'S WORK

Bessie: I'll tell you some other new things we've learned. In our day, men absolutely never did housework, but today you hear about men who help their wives. I say hurray for these men! You know, when we were growing up our brothers would try to cook, but they always made a mess and they weren't very good.

But recently I've seen that men can be excellent cooks. Why about a year ago, we went to a Japanese restaurant. When we got there, they gave us a private room. And there, right in front of us, was the stove. And a *man,* dressed in white with a white hat. He bowed to us, very low, and offered us a choice of chicken, seafood, or beef as the main course. Sadie chose the chicken because it's healthier but, naturally, I ordered the beef. I can't turn down prime rib, no, sir, since Sadie won't let me have it too often at home!

Well, that man cooked right in front of us. He was so agile, so quick, I was just amazed. Why, I never thought I'd live to see the day I'd have some *man* cooking for me.

Sadie: Bessie likes to joke but, truthfully, we've never believed that there was such a thing as "man's work" and "woman's work." Why, Bessie was an excellent dentist, a job that most people considered man's work. That always made her so mad!

I suppose I always liked woman's work. I taught domestic science, what they now call "home economics," but there was plenty of science in it, including the study of vitamins and nutrition and basic principles of health — that didn't make it man's work. I still love to cook, and I could sew beautifully. Those were skills like anything else, and

I was proud of them.

I learned those things well because I was a mama's child — I just adored my mama, and I would follow her around the house and the whole campus, copying everything she did. I guess you could say that Bessie was more of a papa's child. She'd watch Papa fix and build things — he even installed the plumbing and electricity at Saint Aug's — and pretty soon, she could repair things, too. She was always stronger than most women. When the wagon came from town with supplies for Saint Aug's, Bessie would line up with the men to unload it — and I'm talking fifty- and one-hundred-pound bags of things like flour. And she was so good with her hands. Not long ago, she made picture frames for all of our family photos and carved them with lovely leaf and flower designs.

So we think it's silly to worry about man's work and woman's work. Do what makes you happy and be proud of it. But have faith that anything you set your mind to, you can do.

HOMEMAKING

Bessie: So few women had careers in our day that you weren't judged by your achievements outside the home. Instead what mattered were things like the size of the stitches in your sewing — the tinier, the better — and by how light and fluffy you could make your dinner rolls. Well, no one was better than Sadie at that — her dinner rolls were the talk of Harlem! She made all different kinds, but this one was my favorite:

Bessie's Favorite Feather Rolls

5 tablespoons fat from cooking (such as bacon fat)

6 tablespoons plus 1 teaspoon sugar

¾ cup scalded milk

1 package yeast

2 large eggs, beaten

1 teaspoon salt

1 teaspoon lemon juice

¼ teaspoon baking soda

3 cups sifted flour

First, melt the fat and 1 teaspoon of sugar in ¾ cup of milk in a small pan over low heat. Remove it from the heat and then add the 1 package yeast. Let it cool till the surface is bubbly. Move to a large bowl and add the eggs, salt, lemon juice, baking soda, and 6 tablespoons of sugar. Next, add the flour, a cup at a time. You must beat the mixture smooth after each addition. Cover and let it rise until it has doubled in bulk.

Then stir the dough down and, ideally, put it in the icebox overnight. Fill a greased muffin pan half full, and let the dough rise again until it doubles in bulk. Bake at 375 degrees for 15 minutes.

SMALL VANITIES

Sadie: You know, we still enjoy all the little things that go with being women. There's a young woman who helps us out around the house, and every week she does our nails. Since Bessie was a dentist, she has always kept her nails short, and I would never have dreamed of painting mine. But now I regularly wear a fuchsia pink polish that seems to go nicely with my skin, and Bessie's nails are as red as blazes.

Having nice nails is a small thing, but we enjoy it. It's a harmless vanity, and it really cheers us up! We sure appreciate the fact that our helper thought of doing it. That's why Bessie says she's so smart, not only mentally but physically smart.

And here's something you won't believe: Bessie and I just got photographed for a fashion magazine. That's right —

at our age! They wanted to doll us up and take our pictures at some beach in New Jersey. Bessie said, "No, sir, I ain't going to some beach in New Jersey." So the photographer came to us instead, and they fixed up our front yard so it would look like a beach.

We dressed in fine clothes, got our hair done up, and put on a little makeup. We thought we were looking pretty good! And Bessie said, "Sadie, I feel like a little girl again, playing dress-up."

Later we laughed about it. Bessie said, "I think we've gone plumb jack crazy to do what we did today." And I said, "So what? It was fun."

WE AIN'T DEAD YET

Sadie: We're still enjoying menfolks, too! Recently, my doctor said to me, "I have a patient — a man — who is 102 years old. Would you like me to introduce you?" And I said, "No thanks, doctor.

How about somebody your age?"

Then when I was in the hospital with a broken hip, Bessie came to visit me. A man there asked her if she fixed her own hair, and Bessie told him, "Why, yes, I do." "Well, it surely looks nice," he said. Bessie was just tickled to death over that.

Bessie: Well, I'm surely not too old to get crushes on men! One time, Sadie and I were on live television and the host, Regis Philbin, went and kissed me right on the mouth! That shocked me, but someone said, "You sure looked like you enjoyed it!" And I said, "Well, maybe I did and maybe I didn't."

Another time, we were being interviewed on *Good Morning America* and we could not take our eyes off one of the cameramen. He was a tall red-haired man with a handlebar mustache. Finally, I said, "Excuse us for staring, but we haven't seen a mustache like that since Teddy Roosevelt was president!" Later, someone teased us, "Aren't you two something, flirting with that man like that." And I said, "Child, we ain't dead yet!"

We're still making new friends. The world is full of nice folks, if you look for them. Mama used to say, "It's your job to find them." We found Regis Philbin, who surprised us with a kiss on live TV.

9

SOUND OF BODY, PURE OF HEART

THE ORDER OF THE DAY

Bessie: Folks constantly ask about the "secret" that has kept us alive so long. Well, that's something only the Lord can say! We try our best to preserve our health, and one way we do it is to watch what we eat and drink.

We start our day by drinking a full glass of water, followed by a teaspoon of cod liver oil and a whole clove of garlic. A whole, raw clove — that's right. Garlic is good for preventing colds, and it's good for your bowels. We chop the clove as finely as we can, then scoop it up with a spoon, and swallow it all at once, without chewing, to prevent odor. We wash it down with one glass of cold water, then one glass of hot water.

Then we fix our breakfast. In the past few years we've found that breakfast is our most important meal. It's our biggest meal of the day, and we eat it right after we do our exercises. We have a scrambled egg each, a hard roll, and fruit, along with a bowl of oatmeal. I mean home-cooked oatmeal, not that instant stuff.

We have a good meal at midday. Northern folks call that lunch. We southern gals call it dinner. We eat chicken or beef — although we love fish, we don't eat it much today. We worry about its being contaminated. In the evening,

The two of us preparing the garlic; when it comes to health, you can't fool around. Anything worth having in life, you have to work at.

we make ourselves a big vanilla milk shake. It's not good to eat your big meal toward the end of the day.

Every day we take vitamin supplements: vitamin A, B complex, C, D, E, along with zinc and tyrosine. We vary the amount depending on how we've been feeling lately. For example, if I start to get a little tickle in my throat like I am going to get a cold, I take more vitamin C. Antioxidant vitamins are the best. We think it's *best* to get your vitamins naturally, from foods you eat, but supplements are a good idea.

I keep saying "we," but the truth is Sadie's the one in charge of our health. She makes me take my cod liver oil — I can't stand the nasty stuff — and eat what she tells me. If she doesn't think I'm eating enough, she watches me. That just ruins my appetite altogether!

She drives me a little crazy but I guess she's doing something right! I have 103 years of living to show for it.

LIMBER UP!

Sadie: There's another thing I make Bessie do that she doesn't like too much, and that's exercise. You've got to exercise, not just for your heart and lungs, but to keep from stiffening up. It keeps you limber, and that's important when you get older.

We started doing yoga about forty years ago, but don't think we didn't get exercise before that! When we were younger and lived in New York City, we'd walk for miles because we couldn't afford to take the trolley. That was mighty good exercise!

You don't have to get down on the floor and do yoga. You can get exercise from doing housework, gardening, all kinds of things — anything's better than sitting on your behind all day long.

We've been doing exercises every day for about forty years now, and it's part of what keeps us active. Here we're 102 and 100.

GARDEN OF HEALTH

Bessie: Well, I always did prefer gardening to that old yoga. Why, to plant a seed and watch it grow is one of the greatest pleasures of life. We rarely had to buy vegetables because our garden was so lush. In the summer, we'd pick what we wanted to eat for dinner — whatever was ripe — and each fall we'd can a lot of them to eat all winter.

We just know that those vegetables keep us healthy. We make it a point to eat seven different vegetables every day. One way we do it is to cook up dishes that give us all of them at once.

Sadie's Seven Vegetable Casserole

Chop cabbage, turnips, broccoli, carrots, onions, celery, and cauliflower. Layer, one at a time, in a frying pan. Repeat until all the ingredients have been used up. Add a tablespoon of oil. Cook at low heat for 20 minutes.

JUST DESSERTS

Sadie: If you eat a lot of fruit, it will extend your life. Not long ago some fresh bing cherries brought Bessie out of a slump. She was feeling weak, so she ate a bunch before she went to sleep, and you know what? She woke up feeling 100 percent better! She swears it was those bing cherries.

We love fruit, but we've had to cut back on eating citrus fruits because we think they can aggravate rheumatism. But there's one dessert, ambrosia, that we just can't pass up. It was our papa's favorite. Having grown up in Florida, he loved his citrus fruit.

Our family has a funny story about ambrosia. One time, Mama sent ambrosia by train from Raleigh to her parents near Danville, Virginia. We used to do this all the time, but this time there was a delay and the ambrosia started to ferment. Grandma was going to throw it out but our grandfather said, "No, Martha, just put it on the mantelpiece." Oh, he was smart. Every morning he cut off a piece, and he surely did enjoy his ambrosia *liqueur*. It had developed quite a kick!

We always make ambrosia on February 5, Papa's birthday. It's a nice way to remember him.

Ambrosia

Meat of 1 fresh coconut, grated
About 1 dozen oranges
Sugar

First, split open the coconut, peel the black skin inside to remove, and grate the meat with a fine grater; cover it and set aside. Next, peel the oranges, stripping the skin and the white membrane. Slice thinly and discard the seeds. (Mama's short-cut: Peel the oranges, but *don't* remove the white skin. Just slice thinly. Besides, the white skin is good for you.)

In a large serving bowl, place a layer of grated coconut. Follow with a layer of oranges. Then sprinkle on a handful of sugar. Keep repeating these three steps until the bowl is filled, ending with coconut.

Place in the icebox overnight, and spoon into parfait dishes for serving.

YOU CAN'T GIVE UP EVERYTHING

Sadie: It's important to eat healthy, but you won't live a long time unless you indulge yourself every once in a while!

When Bessie gets a little blue, I go in the kitchen and fix and fix and fix until I cook something that old gal can't resist eating. I know all her favorite foods, you know. Nothing works like coconut to cheer up Bessie. Next thing you know, she's her old self, laughing and carrying on. She loves coconut, and that usually does the trick.

Bessie's Fresh Coconut Cookies

½ cup butter
½ cup shortening (e.g., Crisco)
4 tablespoons margarine
2 to 3 cups fresh coconut, grated
2 eggs
1 tablespoon vanilla extract
1 teaspoon lemon extract
3 cups flour
1½ cups sugar
½ teaspoon salt
½ teaspoon mace

Blend butter, shortening, margarine, and coconut. Add the eggs and the vanilla and lemon extracts. Sift the dry ingredients and stir into the coconut mixture. Make into medium-size balls, flatten slightly, and bake at 350 degrees for 20 minutes.

A LITTLE INDULGENCE

Bessie: Alcohol is another little indulgence that's okay, as long as you use it in moderation. It can help you relax and that's good. But we don't go in for that store-bought stuff. Instead, we make our own with the rose petals from our garden.

Sadie's Rose Wine

3 quarts rose petals from the garden
3 quarts boiling water
2 lemons, squeezed and cut up
4 oranges, squeezed and cut up
2 yeast cakes
7 pounds sugar

Take a 1½- to 2-gallon glass or plastic container and fill it with the rose petals (red for good color). Then add 3 quarts of boiling water and let cool overnight. The next day, add the juice and cut-up lemons and oranges and let stand for 3 whole days. Then strain it through cheesecloth. Add yeast cakes, sugar, and enough water to make 2 gallons. Pour into sterilized gallon jugs and cover loosely with cheesecloth or a dish towel. Store in a moderately cool place until fermentation ceases (at least 4, possibly as long as 10, weeks). Then pour into bottles and cork.

CLEAN LIVIN'

Bessie: Water, of course, is the most important drink, and so we're very careful about ours. Why, we'd never dream of drinking it straight from the tap. We boil it first to purify it, then when it cools down, we store it in glass jars.

That's what smart folks did in our day. Another thing we do is wash our hands the minute we walk in the house, the way Mama taught us. She was the cleanest woman alive! When we traveled overnight by train, Mama would get up before dawn to clean the bathroom until it was spotless. How we grumbled when she woke us up, saying, "Girls, hurry up! Get in there before someone else comes along!"

Those habits may sound funny, but they were critical back then, when there were no antibiotics to treat disease. All

169

you could do was prevent it. We figure the world is just as dirty — or worse! — today. Why take a chance on getting sick? We can't remember the last time we had a cold.

Clean livin' — that's what we believe in. And hygiene's only part of it. We also try to stay pure of heart.

10

AIN'T GETTIN'
NO YOUNGER

DON'T ASSUME

Sadie: When you get old, everyone starts to worry about you. They say, "Don't do this, don't do that." It drives us plumb jack crazy. Bessie always says, "If I break my fool neck falling down the stairs while I'm feeding my little dog, well, so be it."

Folks think that because you're old, you're unable to do for yourself. Well, look at us! One time about ten years ago, when we were in our nineties, we needed to move an icebox from storage in the attic to the kitchen. We had hired two men to do it, but days and days passed and they never got around to it. Well, we just up and moved that icebox ourselves. That's right! Me and Bessie. We were slow and careful about it — the hardest part was all those stairs — but we did it. Those two men finally came by and said, "Okay, we're ready to move the refrigerator now." And we said, "You're too late!" They couldn't believe that these two old ladies had moved it themselves. We didn't need those men!

Now I'm not saying that older folks should try to do it all without help. All I mean is that you can't let folks assume that you're nothing but a helpless old fool.

But you do have to be honest about your limitations. If you don't do that, well, your clock's not ticking right!

Sadie: I'm about sixty-five in this picture. The Delany women always looked ten years younger than they were. It's a family trait. Papa used to say, "Well, there's no reason for anyone to know how old you are." He kept our ages out of the family Bible so that no one would peek. All of our brothers kept the secret. They didn't lie, but they always gave the impression that we were their <u>little</u> sisters.

WORRIED TO DEATH

Bessie: It is a nuisance when people keep worrying about us! But I admit that I do tend to worry myself. When Sadie was 103, she broke her left hip and landed in the hospital and, honey, *that's* a situation worth worrying about.

You know, showing up at a hospital at 103 years old, no one wants to touch you. They don't know what to do with old folks, and they just assumed we were senile. They'd talk in front of us like we weren't there. It was mighty insulting.

Well, they finally got a surgeon who would do the operation, which was a success, but Sadie had to stay in the hospital for almost two months. I was just worried to death. I *hated* that hospital. And you know what I hated most? I discovered that the morgue was so close to the kitchen! I'm sort of fanatical about germs, you know. I guess it comes from being a dentist. I like things clean.

But Sadie would say, "Now, Bessie, don't you worry yourself to death. This place isn't going to kill me! Let's just make the best of things." She's smarter than me that way.

Every day she'd remind me, "It's in the Lord's hands, so why fret about it?"

WE DON'T GIVE UP

Sadie: My brightest moment in the hospital was the time Bessie brought my brush and plaited my hair for me. When I looked up, I saw three nurses standing in the doorway, just watching us. I guess they thought it was sweet, this woman over 100 years old brushing her big sister's hair.

I enjoyed that, and I did my best to get along in the hospital. Why, I even learned a few survival tricks. The food was always cold, so I'd order tea, but I didn't plan to drink it. Instead, I'd take the hot water for the tea and spoon it over the food, especially the sauces, to heat it up. It worked like a charm, and I got my hot food. One time the nurses got all upset because they thought I'd disappeared, but I was out in the hallway practicing with my walker. Nobody told me to do that. I just knew I had to take things into my own hands if I was going to get out of that place.

I kept getting roommates who were much younger than me. Funny thing is, I was in a lot better shape than they were! One of them, a lady who was probably in her seventies, was upset and frightened. Nobody came to see her and everyone at the hospital was too busy to pay much attention to her. Well, I decided I would help her, advocate for her. I'd ring the nurse's buzzer for her when she needed something. I'd calm her down when she got scared. And I'd encourage her, saying, "Now, dear, you really must *try*."

That's a big problem with some older folks — they have such low expectations of themselves. When they get to a certain age, they just give up. That's a shame! If there's anything I've learned in all these years, it's that life is too good to waste a day. It's up to you to make it sweet.

SHOW THEM WHO'S THE BOSS

Bessie: When Sadie got home from the hospital, she was very weak, but walking with a walker. So folks thought that for the first time in our lives, we needed help at home. Well, I wasn't about to put up with *that!* I said, "No, sir. There's no one who can take care of Sadie better than I can."

One of my nephews tried to get me to do this and that, but I said, "You run your household; I'll run mine!"

And I did. We managed well for about eight months, and then Sadie broke her *other* hip. Then — can you believe it? — no sooner did Sadie get home than I fell and broke *my* hip. That's right! Now, honey, we're as old as Moses and I guess we should expect these things, but it's mighty hard when your brain works fine and your body is giving out on you.

You know, there's two places I never want to go. One's jail and the other is the hospital! So when the ambulance came for me I told that driver, "Just take me straight to the cemetery. I'd rather go there, yes, sir!"

When I got to the hospital, folks expected that I would behave like Sadie. Honey, that is the story of my life. Ever since I was born, I've been following in Sadie's footsteps. Why, back when we were both teaching, I got a job at one of Sadie's old schools. All I heard was "Sadie does it like this" or "That's not how Sadie did it." Finally I said, "Look, I'm not Sadie. I'm Bessie. And if you don't like it, well, that's just too bad."

The other time I was in the hospital

was way back in 1906, when I got typhoid fever. I was just fifteen years old. But this time, don't worry, I showed those folks who's the boss. Oh, I was *bad*. I'd never let them poke and prod *me!* One day a friend who was visiting noticed my nails had gotten long and offered me a manicure. I said, "No, sir! Don't touch my nails. Why, I just might need these claws!"

Now, I'm not saying the way I carried on was right. All those folks were just trying to help. Sadie gets her way by being sweet and determined but, honey, I don't mince words. If you mess with me, you've got a world of trouble.

But however you do it, you've just got to fight in this life. When you're young, you're busy trying to fight against all the big problems of the world. When you're older, you have to fight to hold on to things like your property and your dignity and your independence.

If there's one thing you've got to hold on to, it's the courage to fight!

1. Keep your own calendar.
The most important thing in your life is your
time, and nothing will make you feel as
helpless as having other people run it for you.

2. Manage your own money, but be careful
about it. Pay your own bills and balance
your checkbook for as long as you can. When
the time comes that someone has to take
a hand in your finances, make sure you
understand everything he does. If other
people take charge of your money, it's easy
to lose control of your life.

3. Have your own doctor, who answers to
you. If you don't, when the time comes that
you get mixed up with hospitals, they'll treat you
like a fool. One time when Sadie was in the
hospital, a technician was taking her blood
pressure, and Sadie simply asked how it was —
good, bad, or indifferent? Why, that girl looked
at her like she was crazy! "Indifferent," she
said, like it was none of Sadie's business.
Well, we solved that problem by getting our
own woman gerontologist. You're bound to
lose your health at some point, but you don't
have to lose your dignity, too.

4. Don't depend too much on any one person. If you have a lot of helpers, you can be sure that someone will always be available when you need it. You'll feel a lot more independent. We have different folks who do different things for us — like give us a ride, go to the post office, or buy our vitamins. By spreading out these little favors, we're not a big burden on anyone.

5. Don't be too proud to accept your limitations. The hardest thing is discovering that you can't do everything the way you used to. We're not happy having folks help us around the house, but we've come to accept it. But make sure you hire folks who do what *you* want. It's still your house, and you're still the boss!

A FEW REGRETS

Bessie: When you get older, it's natural to look back on your life. And like most folks, I have a few regrets. The main regrets I have from 100 years of living come from when I haven't treated someone as well as I could have. When we were children, we used to play near the principal's house on campus at Saint Aug's. His wife, Mrs. Hunter, would come out and very nicely say, "Now, children, Mrs. Hunter has a migraine headache. Please play somewhere else." We'd go off for a while but we always came back to her yard. Looking back, I'm sure we worried that poor woman to death. And you know, I still feel bad about it, after all these years.

And I can be a little mean. Sadie never says anything mean about anyone, especially if they're dead. If I say something mean about someone who's gone to Glory, Sadie will say, "Now, Bessie, of the dead say nothing evil," and I try to be good.

Mama used to tell me, "Bessie, someday you're going to have to account for every mean thing you've ever said." That's what's got me so worried. If I had to do it all over again, I'd hush up once in a while.

Sadie: I know this sounds hard to believe, but I don't have any regrets. I'm the type of person who tends to think before I speak or act, so I don't make so many mistakes . . . or so I hope.

When you get older, you ask yourself, "How have I run my life? Did I live it well?" I think I have. I'm completely satisfied. Maybe all older people should be asked about their lives. When you live a long time, you have stories to tell. If only people ask.

THE LAST WORD

Sadie: This is going to sound kind of crazy to some folks, but we aren't worried about dying one bit. We're hopeful that we'll get to Heaven. And won't it be the greatest pleasure to see Mama and Papa again?

Bessie says she's been to too many funerals in her life. "Next one I go to will be my own," she always says. You see, Bessie feels things deeply. She never stops missing anyone while I just pick up and go on.

She told me recently, "Sadie, I think I'm going to die in my sleep. I think that sounds pretty good." And I said, "Good for *you,* maybe! But what about *me!*" I think that would be a mean thing for her to do to me.

But you know, we aren't ready to give up yet, unless the Lord makes up

His mind that it's finally time to call us. In the meantime, like all human beings, we want to keep on living. As Bessie says, "Heaven is my home but, honey, I ain't homesick!"

When our time comes, we're going to be buried in the family plot in Raleigh. Bessie and I will be buried side by side — right next to Mama and Papa.

We couldn't ask for anything more.

The employees of G.K. HALL hope you have enjoyed this Large Print book. All our Large Print titles are designed for easy reading, and all our books are made to last. Other G.K. Hall Large Print books are available at your library, through selected bookstores, or directly from us. For more information about current and up-coming titles, please call or mail your name and address to:

G.K. HALL
PO Box 159
Thorndike, Maine 04986
800/223-6121
207/948-2962

W9-CKH-011

A GLOSSARY OF
NETSPEAK AND TEXTSPEAK

A Glossary of
Netspeak and Textspeak

David Crystal

Edinburgh University Press

© David Crystal, 2004

Edinburgh University Press Ltd
22 George Square, Edinburgh

Typeset in Sabon
by Hewer Text Ltd, Edinburgh, and
printed and bound in Finland by
WS Bookwell

A CIP record for this book is
available from the British Library

ISBN 0 7486 2119 9 (hardback)
ISBN 0 7486 1982 8 (paperback)

Contents

Introduction

This glossary is an example of a new kind of reference publication – what I call a *lexipedia*. The name reflects its purpose: it is a cross between a dictionary (or lexicon) and an encyclopaedia. It brings together some of the information about words which is included in a dictionary and the sort of knowledge which you would expect to find in an encyclopaedia.

The book has two aims. First, it is a guide to the rapidly emerging jargon associated with the Internet and its use, and to the associated terminology of mobile communications. Second, it provides definitions and examples of the way this terminology has been adopted by young (or young-minded) Internet users and adapted for use in non-Internet settings. The words have therefore begun to make their appearance in the language as a whole – though usually only as part of the slang of colloquial speech.

I have concentrated on the terms I have heard used or seen onscreen. My examples of original usage all reflect what I have found in search-engine sites (such as Google) with a good lexical indexing system, though I have changed a few names to ensure anonymity. I have not, however, tried to reflect frequency of use. Some of my examples are very common; others much less so. In 2003 there were over 4 million instances of *download* in the Google database, for example, but only 500 instances of *gronked*.

My guide is not a frequency guide, accordingly, but an

illustration of the sort of thing that is currently happening 'out there'. As is typical of slang, several of the words have varying usage, and their meanings are prone to change with fashion. Some of the usages I am recording may die out in due course, but others may grow in popularity, and may eventually enter the standard language. It is never possible to predict the future, with language change.

Some things I have not included. There is a tendency for people in chatrooms, game-environments and computing laboratories to develop a consciously idiosyncratic (not to say eccentric) vocabulary, which acts as a badge of identity for a particular group. It is notoriously transient and local in character, and I have steered clear of it, concentrating on words which are more widespread. I have also avoided basic computing terminology, except when I needed a term to help explain an Internet usage. And my list does not include the names of commercial operations, such as the various search engines or mobile-phone companies.

What is surprising, in a way, is that this book is so small. The Internet has not yet had a major impact on English vocabulary and use. Perhaps this is not surprising, given that it has been in existence only for a generation – an eyeblink, in terms of language chronology. But when words do begin to come into general use, what the Internet does is spread the words around the globe faster than has ever been possible before. 'The chief use of slang', it has often been said, 'is to show that you're one of the gang.' This still obtains, but today the Internet lets us be members of a global gang.

My thanks to Tony McNicholl for help in preparing the database structure that I used for this project, and also for researching some of the usage in mobile communications. Thanks too to Ben and Lucy Crystal for letting me use their young intuitions to check the observations of this not-so-young (but definitely young-minded) linguist.

David Crystal

An A-to-Z of Netspeak

The alphabetical arrangement of the A-to-Z section is letter by letter. Terms beginning with a number (such as *2G*, *404*) are located in their alphabetical place (*2* = two, *4* = four, etc.).

A

A-band (US) >> **B-band**

abort To stop a computer program while it is running, often shown by an **abort message** onscreen. This action can be initiated by the computer itself, having detected a fault, or by the user deliberately wanting to cancel an operation.
ORIGINAL USE
(as a verb) *Something in the system aborted what I was doing, and I lost my page.*
(as a noun) *I get an abort every time I try to print my file.*
NEW USE
(as a verb) stop, cancel [an action]
I wanted to go to the party – No, abort that! – Joan asked me to go to the party.
(as a noun) breakdown, failure
I think there's going to be an abort in that relationship before too long.

access To reach data stored in a computer, or to send data to a computer; also, the ability to reach or send such data.
ORIGINAL USE

(as a verb) *I can't access the data without a password.*
(as a noun) *That password worked; I've got access now.*
NEW USE
(as a verb) grasp, fully understand
I'm having trouble accessing what you just said. Go over it again, would you?

access fee A fee that traditional phone companies charge to mobile users for the right to connect with the local phone network. >> mobile phone; network

access point In mobile communications, the interface between the wireless network and the wired network. >> mobile communications; network

access time The length of time required to retrieve information from computer memory or other computer storage media, such as magnetic disks or tapes. Access times from integrated circuit memory are much shorter than those from magnetic disks. >> memory

ack An abbreviation of *acknowledge*, sent in reply to a message to show that it has been received.
EXTENDED USE
(as an interjection) used to interrupt someone to show that a point is understood and that it is unnecessary to continue; often repeated two or three times
Speaker A: Well, Jane turned up at Mike's house a bit early, and as a result – B: Ack, ack, I'm with you.
RELATED USE
Nak, used as an interruption to show that a point has not been understood, and that some clarification is needed
Speaker A: Get the train from Euston, but you'll need to change at Reading – B: Nak, nak, Reading? Not from Euston, surely?

ADSL >> Asymmetric Digital Subscriber Line

Advanced Mobile Phone System (AMPS) An analogue system developed in the USA and Canada in the early 1980s, operating in the 824–894 Mhz frequency range, and still in use. >> analogue; megahertz

aerial >> antenna

-age A suffix which makes a noun more abstract, expressing such notions as 'measure of' or 'collection of' (as in *mileage, luggage*) or which turns a verb into a noun (as in *coverage*). Examples of Internet coinages are *nettage, flamage, winnage* and *lossage*. >> flamage; loss

airtime or **talktime** In mobile communications, the duration of a call, normally measured in seconds. Network operators have many different methods of charging for airtime and type of call (voice, data, sending or receiving, Short Messaging Service, fax) with periods of free airtime offered as part of a contract. >> all inclusive; mobile phone; network; pay as you go; pay monthly; pay up front; reverse billing

A-Key >> authentication

all inclusive In mobile communications, a term describing an account where the fees and service charges involved in using a phone are calculated for the year, and, in return for prepayment, which is normally divided into monthly instalments, discounts are offered on the purchase of equipment, and a quantity of monthly free airtime is included. Some contracts allow unused free time to be carried forward from month to month. >> mobile phone

alpha A term describing the early stage in the in-house project development of a piece of software or hardware. >> beta
ORIGINAL USE
(as an adjective) *It took over a year before they gave XJQ an alpha release.*
(as a noun) *XJQ is currently in alpha.*
NEW USE
(as an adjective) tentative, cautious, speculative
I've not got very far yet with Phil. I'm only at an alpha stage in that relationship.
(as a noun) exploratory stage, tentative approach
Got beyond alpha yet with Phil?

alpha geek The most knowledgeable or technically aware person in a computer research environment. >> geek
ORIGINAL USE
John was the alpha geek in the Xios set-up for several years.
NEW USE
most important person, person in charge
I want to know what happened to my memo. Who's the alpha geek in this department?
most knowledgeable person, most proficient player
[advertisement] *Subscribe to our weekly mag and you can be the alpha geek when the talk turns to racing cars.*

alphanumeric A set of characters which includes all the lower- and upper-case letters of the alphabet (*a* to *z*, *A* to *Z*), the digits *0* to *9*, and some punctuation characters; also, a device that can input or display this set of characters. >> numeric

alt., pronounced /alt dot/ A Usenet newsgroup devoted to an unorthodox or entertaining topic. >> Usenet

ORIGINAL USE
(as a prefix) *I spent hours last night talking to some guys on alt.life.sucks.*
NEW USE
(as an adjective) alternative, unorthodox
I've been doing some alt. thinking about our problem.
(also, as an adjective) cool, way-out, hip
That's an alt. way of looking at things.

American Standard Codes for Information Interchange >> ASCII

AMPS >> Advanced Mobile Phone System

analog (US, and increasingly general) or **analogue** (UK) A term describing an information transmission system where the information is represented by a continuously varying quantity such as voltage. In mobile communications, for example, the first cellular systems were analogue, but these have largely been superseded by digital systems. >> cell; digital; mobile phone
ORIGINAL USE
(as an adjective) [advertisement] *This analog clock also has a digital time display and a chime!*
NEW USE
(as an adjective) difficult, complicated
Go back a bit – that point's too analog for me to handle.
inefficient, cumbersome
Faxing is a very analog way of reaching Jane. I always email her.
(also, as an adjective) out-dated, old-fashioned
He's analog – he still reads novels!

angle brackets Brackets which have developed an additional range of functions in some genres of Internet communication. In email dialogues, a right-pointing bracket is introduced by some email software to identify the lines of a message to which someone is replying. Pairs of angle brackets surround tags in markup languages, identify descriptive statements in some chatgroup dialogues (e.g. <David laughs quietly>), and demarcate the string of symbols that constitutes an Internet address (such as <info@crystalreference.com>). >> chatgroup; email; markup language

anonymizer A device which impedes or prevents the electronic traceability of messages on a computer network. Techniques include the use of pseudonyms, encryption systems, remailing services which disguise a message source, and free email services which do not check the user's personal details. An **anonymous remailer**, for example, strips the identifying information out of an email header, transmitting only the message. >> email; header

antenna The component of a radio system by which electromagnetic signals are transmitted or received; also known as the **aerial**. In mobile communications, early phones had an antenna which had to be extended before the phone could be used; most now have a built-in antenna. >> mobile phone

antimailbomb >> **mailbomb**

applet A short program, written in a language such as JAVA, which can be called from a Web document while the document is being processed by a browser. When the applet is called, it is downloaded from the Web site and run in the user's computer. The JAVA language has been designed to allow applets to operate in users' computers without presenting a threat to security. >> browser; download; Web

arch >> **wizard**

archive >> **log**

article A term sometimes used for a message sent by an email system to a chatgroup or other online forum. The more common term is **post.** >> post

ASCII (pron: /**as**kee/) An acronym for the **American Standard Code for Information Interchange,** a code for representing English characters as numbers. ASCII-96, an 8-bit code including a parity check bit, is the most common code in use for storing text character strings in computers. In the standard set, characters 0 through 127 allows 96 printing characters to be defined (letters, digits, arithmetical symbols and punctuation marks) together with a number of control characters, such as printer carriage return and halt processing. An enlarged system, called **extended ASCII** or **high ASCII,** is also available, allowing further characters to be introduced (numbers 128 through 255). >> ASCII art; binary code; parity check

ASCII art An artistic construction made up out of the symbols in the ASCII code. Email signatures sometimes contain such a composition as part of the sender's identity. >> ASCII; email

asterisk (*) A traditional punctuation mark, which has been given extra functions in electronic communication; also sometimes referred to colloquially as a *star*, *splat*, *dingle*, *spider*, *aster* and *twinkle*. It is a widely used way of showing emphasis (e.g. *that is a *very* important point*). In some chatgroups, a single asterisk signals an action or comment by a participant (e.g. **DC is confused*), and a triple asterisk (* * *) identifies a message from the software system as opposed to a message from a participant (e.g. ***DC has joined this channel*). In computing, the asterisk is used as a wildcard in carrying out searches. >> chatgroup; email; punctuation; wildcard

Asymmetric Digital Subscriber Line (ADSL) A development in telecommunications that enables digital data transfer over conventional copper-wire telephone lines at speeds up to 2 Mbps (almost 40 times as fast as a conventional 56K modem) with simultaneous voice use. The service is assymmetric, as download speed is much greater than upload speed. >> broadband; download; Mbps; modem

asynchronous (1) A term describing chatgroups where the discussions do not take place in real time. An example of such a group is a bulletin board, where messages can be posted at any time and left for others to read at any other time. >> chatgroup; Usenet; WELL **(2)** More generally, in telecommunications, describing data which can be transmitted at any time, such as a voicemail message. >> voicemail

at (@) In email addresses, the universally used symbol for linking recipient and address. Although the symbol is universal, its name varies vividly among languages, e.g. 'snail' in Italian, 'little mouse' in Chinese. >> email

attachment A file of data accompanying the text of an email. >> email

atto- The standard SI (International System of Units) prefix expressing ten to the power of negative 18.
ORIGINAL USE
(as a prefix) [news report] *A technology has been developed to measure atto-newton forces – a billionth of a billionth of a newton.*

NEW USE
(as an adjective) unimaginably useless, totally irrelevant, much worse than zero
Taking another course is of atto interest to me right now.

authentication (1) In mobile communications, a fraud prevention technology that takes a number of values – including a 26-character handset identifier, or **A-Key**, which is not sent over the air – to create a shared secret value which can verify a user's authenticity. >> mobile phone (2) In Internet communication, a technical procedure which verifies the identity of a sender in an email or other electronic dialogue. Web sites which are **authenticated** require users to register their identities before being allowed access. >> email; Web

avatar The onscreen visual identity adopted by someone entering the environment of a virtual world. Avatars are usually pictorial (such as a cartoon character) but may be text-based. >> character; virtual world

B

background The electronic domain behind the active area of a screen where another computational process is ongoing; an email, for example, might be received *in background* while a piece of text is being edited on screen. The term can also be used to describe a process which is taking place in this way, as in the case of *background printing*.
ORIGINAL USE
(as a noun) *You don't have to interrupt what you're doing – just print the pages in background.*
NEW USE
(as a noun) secondary position, less important task

I'm a bit busy right now, but I'll certainly keep plugging away at it in background.
(as a verb) postpone, put on the back burner
I'll background thinking about his letter until I get a bit of spare time.
RELATED USE
foreground (as a verb) deal with, bring to the forefront of attention
I'd appreciate it if you'd foreground that memo as soon as you can.

backspace A key which deletes the character to the left of the cursor and moves the cursor one space to the left (unless the cursor is at the first position in the input line, in which case the key has no effect).
ORIGINAL USE
(as a noun) *Press backspace and you'll get rid of the error.*
(as a verb) *Backspace three times and you'll delete the word 'but'.*
NEW USE
(as a verb) hold on, wait, go back,
Hey, backspace a minute! I want to go over that again.

backup, back-up, back up A computing procedure which avoids data loss or corruption. Copies of data files, disks, etc. are created and stored separately from the original, so that they may be restored in the event of a problem.

bagbiter A piece of hardware or software that fails to work or that works very inefficiently; also said of the person who built the hardware or programmed the software. An expletive form, **bagbiting,** is also used as an intensifying adjective, referring to the worthlessness of the entitities or people involved in such cases.

ORIGINAL USE

(as a noun) *I'm totally fed-up with that system. It's a real bagbiter!*

(as an intensifier) *If that bagbiting machine lets me down again, it's on the rubbish-heap!*

NEW USE

(as a noun) idiot, loser

Fred got lost on the way home, as always, poor old bagbiter.

(as an intensifier) worthless, useless

Mary keeps sending me these bagbiting invitations to win a free holiday.

band A range of adjacent frequencies in an electromagnetic signal. >> bandwidth; broadband; dual band; tri-band

bandwidth In acoustics, the interval between two given limits within which a range of frequencies falls. The notion defines the capacity of a channel to carry information without distortion. >> bandwidth hog; bandwidth junkie; broadband

ORIGINAL USE

(as a noun) *To send sound as well as colour would require a much greater bandwidth.*

NEW USE

(as a noun) brain-power, mental capacity, ability to take something on

I need more bandwidth to handle that point. (= I can't take it all in at once)

Wish I could help, but no bandwidth, sorry.

RELATED USE

narrow/low bandwidth, wide/high bandwidth

You'll have to speak slowly, he's narrow bandwidth! (= he can't cope with too much information at a time)

When it comes to computer games, she's a real high-bandwidth type. (= she can handle any technical point you throw at her)

Don't waste your bandwidth listening to him. (= he's talking nonsense)

synonym: **brainwidth**

Don't waste your brainwidth listening to him. (= he's talking nonsense)

bandwidth hog In data transmission, something which uses up the capacity of a channel (such as a video file), not allowing other data to get through. The analogy is with *road hog.*

ORIGINAL USE

You'll find that fancy graphics package is an absolute bandwidth hog.

NEW USE

(as a noun) person who keeps sending too much unwanted information, especially electronically

He's become a real bandwidth hog since joining that campaign. (= he's always sending messages about it to everyone)

RELATED USE

bandwidth hogging greedy use of a channel

He's doing a lot of bandwidth hogging these days.

bandwidth junkie Someone who is obsessed with downloading information at the fastest possible rate; someone who browses the Web at high speed; someone who can't stop surfing the Web. >> bandwidth; browser; surf; Web

bang A spoken name for the exclamation mark when it is used onscreen, especially as part of a programmer's language.

ORIGINAL USE

Line 27 reads O bang A bang 402.

NEW USE
(as an interjection) typically used to express sudden mental enlightenment, 'light dawning'
Bang! Got it! She must have known who the murderer was!

barney Someone who has a passing interest in using the Internet or one of its applications, and who is thus not very proficient. >> newbie
ORIGINAL USE
(as a noun) *I think we've got a barney in the class who's slowing things down for everyone else.*
NEW USE
(as a noun) clueless individual, scatterbrain
This barney was just sitting there, on his mobile, with no idea that the lights had changed.

barring >> call barring

base station In mobile communications, a site containing a radio transmitter/receiver and network communication equipment. >> cell; network

batch A number of items collected by a computer over a period of time. In **batch processing**, a set of data collected in this way is dealt with in a single computational operation.
ORIGINAL USE
(as a noun or adjective)
[advertisement] *XXX lets you make a batch download direct from the Web.*
NEW USE
(as an adjective) ready to do routine tasks
Show me the cleaning things. I'm in batch mode today!
RELATED USE
batch up to accumulate a series of tasks to be carried out in one go

I've batched up all the garden jobs for tomorrow, so I hope it's fine.

baud A unit used to measure the capacity of a communications channel to carry digital data; named after French electrical engineer Jean-Maurice-Emile Baudot (1845–1903). The **baud rate** of a communications channel is the number of signal changes per second with which the channel can cope.

B-band (US) In mobile communications, a type of licence which protects consumers against possible anti-competitive practice. Two sets of mobile operator licences have been issued. The first set went automatically to the local landline telephone companies, usually a regional Bell operating company, hence 'B' band. The alternative licence ('A' band) was drawn for in a lottery and often sold on later by the lottery winner. >> mobile phone

BBS >> bulletin board system

Bcc >> Cc

beta A term describing the stage where a project is sufficiently advanced to be given a public (but not commercial) release, so that any remaining bugs can be eliminated. >> alpha
ORIGINAL USE
(as an adjective) *XJQ has got a beta release now.*
(as a noun) *XJQ is currently in beta.*
NEW USE
(as an adjective) experimental, new, exploratory
I can see all sorts of beta possibilities in John and Mary's relationship.
(as an adjective) dubious, suspect

Ted came out with some really beta thoughts on the future of Europe.

bicapitalization (BiCaps) or **intercaps, incaps, midcaps** The spelling of a compound word with two capital letters, one at the beginning and the other where the second part of the compound begins. It is a feature of Internet graphology, especially encountered in business names and products, such as *AltaVista*, *PostScript*, *PeaceNet* and *AskJeeves*. Cases of more than two capitals are included under the same heading, as in *QuarkXPress*. >> Internet

BiCaps >> bicapitalization

binary code A code derived from the binary number system, using only two digits (0 and 1), in comparison with the decimal system, which has ten digits (0 to 9). The advantage of the binary system for use in digital computers is that only two electronic states, off and on, are required to represent all the possible binary digits. All digital computers operate using various binary codes to represent numbers, characters, etc. >> ASCII code; bit

bit In computing, an abbreviation of **Binary digIT**, a computational quantity with only two possible values in the binary number system, 0 or 1. All operations in digital computers and other electronic digital devices take place by using a high or low voltage (an 'on' or 'off' state) to represent the binary digits. >> binary code; bitloss
ORIGINAL USE
(as a noun) *A bit is the smallest unit that can be stored in computer memory.*
NEW USE
(as a singular noun) quick piece of information, yes/no response

Can I have a bit from you about whether we should publish the new rotas?
(as a plural noun) pieces of information, data
I need some bits about how we're doing in Europe.
RELATED USE
bit flip complete change of direction in life
Don't try calling John. He's in the middle of a bit flip and isn't answering the phone.
bit set number of points held in mind
Have you got five minutes? I have a bit set for you about the meeting tomorrow.

bit flip >> bit

bitloss The loss of data bits during a transmission. >> bit
ORIGINAL USE
(as a noun) *The rates of bitloss in mobile communications can be a real problem.*
NEW USE
(as a noun) loss of memory, mental block
Sorry, I'm suffering from bitloss – I'll remember his name in a minute.

bit set >> bit

blackholing A technique for denying a route to your computer for messages from a particular Internet address. It is commonly used in the automatic deletion of spam mail. >> Internet; spam

blackspot or **deadspot** An area of poor coverage for mobile communications, often caused by the nature of the terrain (high ground between transmitter and receiver) or physical location, such as in subways. >> mobile phone

blind courtesy/carbon copy >> Cc

blog An abbreviation for **Weblog** or **Web log**, an individual's frequently updated mixture of personal observation, commentary and links posted as a Web page; the person who maintains such a log is a **blogger**, and the activity is known as **blogging**. Blogs, which first came to notice in 1999, were originally pages presenting a personal selection or filtering of links to little-known sites on the Web, with an accompanying editorial commentary. But commercial interfaces soon developed (such as Blogger), making it very easy for an individual with minimal technical expertise to send material to a site, and the genre quickly took on the character of a diary or journal. Most blogs are now diarial in intention, with new material added frequently at the top of the page. Thematic blog domains have also evolved, in the manner of chatgroups, such as **flogs** (food logs). >> chatgroup

Bluetooth An open standard for wireless communication over short distances between mobile and desktop devices. It operates in the 24 Ghz band, has a range of 10 m up to 100 m with power boost, and a maximum data transfer rate of 720 Kbps. It was first developed by the Scandinavian company Ericsson, and is named after the Danish Viking Harald Bluetooth. >> hertz; Kbps

bogon, pronounced /**boh**gon/ [from *bogus*, on analogy with *electron*, etc.] A piece of software that does not function properly; also, an incorrectly formed packet sent on a network.
ORIGINAL USE
We've put a filter in to try and reduce the flow of bogons.
NEW USE
(as a noun) pointless activity, waste of time

Once a month we have a ridiculous bogon with the so-called quality assurance team.
(as a noun) person who is a time-waster, phoney
You don't want to waste your time talking to that bogon.

bookmark To add the address of a Web site of particular interest to a list in one's own computer, thereby allowing the user to visit the site rapidly. The listed sites are also called **bookmarks** (or **favorites/favourites**). >> Web
ORIGINAL USE
(as a verb) *That's a really interesting site. I think I'll bookmark it.*
NEW USE
(as a verb) store away for future reference, make a mental note
Good point! I'll bookmark that for the next time I see her.

bot A program designed to carry out a particular task; derived from *robot*: a *spellbot*, for example, might be devised to check a text's spelling. Bots are usually identified through compounds, where the first part of the word hints at the function to be performed, as in *annoybot, chatterbot, knowbot, cancelbot, softbot, mailbot* and *spybot*.

bounce or **bounce back** The return of an email to its sender by a server to which it had been sent. This usually happens because there has been some error in the e-address, but other causes of failure to deliver also occur, such as the address having been changed or no longer existing. >> email; server
ORIGINAL USE
(as a verb) *My message to Tim has bounced. I'd better check the address.*
NEW USE
(as a verb) ignore, reject
I'd say hello, but I'm scared she might bounce me.

bps An abbreviation for **bits per second,** referring to the rate of data transmission. >> bit; Kbps; Mbps

braindump, brain-dump An account of everything one knows about a particular subject in computing. >> core-dump

ORIGINAL USE

(as a noun) *Can you give me a braindump on model HK2?*

NEW USE

(as a noun) speaking at length on a subject without considering what the listener wants or needs to hear

I just mentioned Mark, and Mary spent five minutes giving me a braindump on him!

(as a verb) talk at length, go on obsessively

She turned up at seven, braindumped at me about her new boss for half an hour, then left.

brainwidth >> **bandwidth**

broadband A general term describing data transmission speeds above those found in the standard telephone network. Figures range from above 1.5 Mbs to above 45 Mbs. **broadband ISDN (B-ISDN)** is a data communications service developed by telecommunications agencies throughout the world to allow data to be transferred digitally at very high speed over optical networks. Baud rates of 600 Mbps (megabauds per second) were introduced in the 1990s, with much higher rates to follow. More recently, the term has been applied to high-speed Internet access via the existing copper telephone network, using ADSL technology. >> Asymmetric Digital Subscriber Line; band; baud; Mbps; Integrated Services Digital Network

browser A type of computer program which uses the Internet to locate and transfer documents held on Web sites, and presents the documents to the user of the program in a way which makes them easy to read and understand. The two most commonly used browers are Netscape Communicator and Microsoft Internet Explorer. >> HTML browser; Internet; Web

brute force A method of solving a programming problem by trying all possible solutions until the right one is found.
ORIGINAL USE
We'll try brute force as a routine to crack that password.
NEW USE
trying out all possible methods [to arrive at a solution of any problem]
I'll get a ticket to the concert through brute force, you wait and see!

buffer A temporary storage area in memory for data. Buffers are often used when transmitting data between two devices with different working speeds, such as between a keyboard and the central processor, or the central processor and a printer. >> buffer overflow
ORIGINAL USE
(as a noun) *If you send the document to the printer now, it'll hold it in its buffer until it's ready to print it.*
NEW USE
(as a noun) brain capacity, mental-processing ability
I forgot to write to the tax office – my buffer trying to cope with too many things, as usual.

buffer overflow or **buffer overload** Loss of data through trying to store more data in a buffer than it can handle. >> buffer

ORIGINAL USE
There are a number of buffer-overflow vulnerabilities in that software.
NEW USE
problem in assimilating, difficulty in remembering
Sorry, but I'm having a bit of a buffer overflow here. Could you run through that again?
RELATED USE
blow one's buffer lose a train of thought
I've completely blown my buffer – where was I up to?

bug An error in a computer program or a fault in computer hardware. The process of detecting and correcting errors is known as **debugging**. >> feature, it's a
ORIGINAL USE
(as a noun) *They haven't eliminated all the bugs in the latest software release.*
NEW USE
(as a noun) hang-up, personality problem
I'm afraid Jim still has a few bugs when it comes to dealing directly with clients.

bulletin board or **bulletin board system (BBS)** A form of electronic notice board in data communications networks, particularly those linking academic institutions. The bulletin board hosts such messages as notices of meetings, technical papers and requests for assistance. >> asynchronous; chatgroup

byte A fixed number of bits (binary digits), usually defined as a set of 8 bits. An 8-bit byte can therefore take 256 different values corresponding to the binary numbers 00000000, 00000001, 00000010, through to 11111111. >> bit; gigabyte; kilobyte; megabyte

C

call barring In mobile communications, a feature offered by a service provider which allows the user to stop either outgoing or incoming calls; often referred to simply as **barring**. >> mobile phone

call divert In mobile communications, a feature offered by a service provider which allows the user to redirect a call either to another phone number or to voicemail; often referred to simply as **divert**. >> mobile phone; voicemail

caller ID In telecommunications, a feature that displays a caller's phone number on the receiver's handset.

call holding In telecommunications, a feature offered by a service provider which allows the user to put a call on hold so that another call can be answered; also referred to simply as **holding**. >> service provider

capital letters The set of upper-case letters, which have developed an additional range of associations in email and chatgroup communication. In particular, messages which are completely in capitals are considered to be 'shouting', and are generally avoided unless the sender is making a point. Because of the extra effort involved in typing an upper-case character, messages often avoid them altogether – a convention which has attracted criticism from conservative users, who believe that an important dimension of linguistic expression is thereby being lost. In fact, the amount of ambiguity that actually arises from the omission of capitals is minimal. >> flame

card >> **Wireless Markup Language**

Cc A space within an email header which contains addresses (other than that of the primary recipient) to which a copy of the email can be sent; often glossed as **courtesy copy** (though etymologically the abbreviation stands for *carbon copy*). A further space can be made available for addresses to which a copy is to be sent without the primary recipient's knowledge: this is designated **Bcc** (for **blind courtesy/carbon copy**). >> email; header

cell In mobile communications, the geographical area where signals from a transmitter can be received. Mobile phone networks are typically made up of many cells, each operating on a discrete frequency that will not interfere with those in use in adjacent cells. The size of a cell is determined by population density: high density areas have a large number of small cells with low-power transmitters, whereas a sparsely populated area will have few cells covering a much larger area with higher-power transmitters. In a *cellular* network, a signal can be passed between cells, as a mobile-phone conversation moves about; in a *non-cellular* network, phones are linked to a single (more powerful) transmitter. >> base station; hand off; mobile phone

cell info display In mobile communications, a feature which enables a phone user to see the reference or cell global identity number of the current cell in use. >> cell

cellphone, cell phone >> **mobile phone**

cellular >> **mobile phone**

Cellular Telecommunications and Internet Association (CTIA) A US association founded in 1984 to represent all elements of the wireless communication industry to the

Federal Communications Commission. >> Federal Communications Commission

character In virtual-world environments, an onscreen persona created by a participant, with its own name and associated description; also called an **avatar**. Several alternative characters (or **morphs**) may belong to a single participant. If a participant stops role-playing but continues to communicate with other members, that person is said to be **out-of-character** (**OOC**). The offscreen human controller of a persona is usually called, straightforwardly, a **typist**. >> avatar; virtual world

chat A mobile-phone messaging service offered by some service providers which enables users with suitably equipped phones to engage in point-to-point messaging between two users, or multi-point chat with several users simultaneously. It is also possible to access some Internet chat sites. >> chatgroup; messaging; mobile phone

chatgroup, chat group A group of people who meet regularly at a particular Internet site (a **chatroom** or **chat room**) to discuss topics of common interest. Most chats take place in real time (they are *synchronous*), but it is possible to carry on a conversation in an *asynchronous* way, where the messages are stored for later scrutiny, as with bulletin boards and mailing lists. Terminology varies greatly: for example, Usenet sites are known as **newsgroups** (or **groups**); sites belonging to the Well (Whole Earth 'Lectronic Link) are known as **conferences**. Other terms referring to types of Internet meeting include **usergroups**, **discussion lists** and **e-conferences**. >> bulletin board; Internet; Internet Relay Chat; mailing list; smurf; Usenet; WELL

chatroom, chat room >> chatgroup

chip or **microchip** A commonly used name for an integrated circuit. Strictly, the term refers to the small 'chip' of silicon on which the electronic circuits reside, rather than the encapsulated package.

ORIGINAL USE

(as a noun) *I think there must be something wrong with the chip controlling the monitor display.*

NEW USE

(as a noun) brain circuit, mental process

Are you listening to me? Are all your chips functioning?

click To press a key on a computer mouse so that the computer is instructed to perform a particular activity.

ORIGINAL USE

(as a verb) *If you click on that symbol, the page should come up straight away.*

NEW USE

(as a noun) very short distance

They're just a click away from getting together.

client/server The relationship between a personal computer (or **client**) and the central computer (or **server**) to which it is linked. The terms refers to the machines themselves (or the software they run), and not to the computer users. >> server

ORIGINAL USE

(as an adjective) *You will find details of the client/server software architecture on page 3 of this manual.*

NEW USE

(as an adjective) as lovers, sexually intimate

I hear that Ted and Tina have developed a nice client/server relationship.

CMC >> computer-mediated communication

codec An acronym for **coder/decoder,** a device for converting the analogue signals used by audio and video equipment to digital form so that the signals can be sent over digital telecommunications networks such as ISDN. >> Integrated Services Digital Network

computer-mediated communication (CMC) A name often given to the kind of language used when people talk to each other using electronic means, such as in email and chatgroups. >> chatgroup; email

conference >> **chatgroup**

content provider A company that specializes in providing data on real-world topics to anyone who needs it (especially Web sites). Any conceivable subject-matter falls under the heading of 'content', from poems to enyclopaedias. >> content service; Web

content service In mobile communications, a paging service which goes beyond telephone-number alerts to include all kinds of content, such as news and sports headlines, personalized stock quotes, driving directions and restaurant reviews. >> content provider; mobile phone; pager

cookie A unique identifier that a Web server places on a computer's hard disk, enabling the originating Web site to keep a record of who has visited the site, and of the user's preferences, such as the site pages accessed or queries made. Cookie protection software is available, for those concerned about the protection of privacy.
ORIGINAL USE
(as a noun) *When you close your browser, the cookie will not be erased from memory.*

(as a verb) *I reckon I've been cookied hundreds of times.*
(= had cookies placed on my disk)
NEW USE
(as a noun) identifying object, visiting card
Jean wasn't in, so I stuck a little cookie on her car windscreen so that she'd know I'd called.

coredump, core dump In early computer technology, a copy or print-out of the entire contents in a computer's memory (RAM), carried out usually to assist in a debugging operation. Because everything is copied, regardless of whether the information is relevant to a particular enquiry or not, a contrast can be drawn with a *braindump*, where the information tends to be more restricted and more focused; but the two terms are often used synonymously. >> braindump

ORIGINAL USE
(as a noun) *That line tells us what the machine was doing when the core dump was made.*
NEW USE
(as a noun) *I only asked for a newspaper, and I got a core dump on the economy.*
RELATED USE
dump core ramble on interminably
He dumped core on me for nearly an hour.

country code >> **top-level domain**

courtesy copy >> **Cc**

coverage area In mobile communications, the geographical area covered by a network service provider; known as a **Public Land Mobile Network** area (**PLMN**) in the GSM (Global System for Mobile Communication) network. >> Global System for Mobile Communication; network

cracker >> hacker

crash The sudden total failure of a computer program or a
   piece of computer hardware; also, to fail in this way.
   ORIGINAL USE
   (as a noun) *Every time I get a crash I lose so much time.*
   (as a verb) *That's the second time today my machine's
   crashed.*
   NEW USE
   (as an intransitive verb) break down, stop, give up
   *John did his best to keep talking, but he just lost the thread
   and crashed.*
   (as a transitive verb) cause to break down, make stop
   *Don't sit at the front of the hall while I'm talking, or you'll
   crash me.*

crunch To use a computer to process a large amount of data,
   especially of a relatively trivial kind.
   ORIGINAL USE
   (as a verb) *It should take my machine about two hours to
   crunch all the departure times.*
   NEW USE
   (as a verb) take in, assimilate
   *You're not expecting me to crunch all those names, are
   you?*
   (as a verb) process, handle
   *I'm crunching your order right now. I should have it
   ready by lunchtime.*

**CTIA >> Cellular Telecommunications and Internet Associa-
   tion**

cuspy Term describing a program which has been very well
   written and gives excellent performance; derived from the
   acronym of *commonly used system program.*

ORIGINAL USE
(as an adjective) *John has come up with a really cuspy solution to the difficulty I had in running that program.*
NEW USE
(as an adjective) beautiful, attractive, excellent
There's a really cuspy secretary just joined the marketing department.

cyber- A prefix designating an entity, event, or other phenomenon which relates to the electronic space (*cyberspace*) within which the Internet and other networks function. Hundreds of coinages have emerged since the 1980s, such as *cybercafe, cyberculture, cyberlawyer, cybersex, cybersquatter, cyberian* and *cyber rights*. >> cyberspace; Internet; network

cyberspace The world of information present or possible in digital form; also called the **information superhighway**. >> Internet

cyberspeak >> Netspeak

D

data services >> General Packet Radio System

DDL >> document description language

dead link A supposedly genuine hypertext link on the Web which turns out to be spurious. An error message is returned saying that a page or site could not be found. Reasons include the removal of a page from a site or a site closing down. >> 404 error; hypertext link; Web

deadspot >> blackspot

debugging >> bug

deck >> Wireless Markup Language

DECT >> Digital Enhanced Cordless Telecommunications

deleted folder A location in an email facility which lists the received emails that the user no longer wishes to keep, and from where they can be permanently deleted. >> email

DGPS >> Global Positioning System

Differential GPS >> Global Positioning System

digital A term describing any method of representing information (numbers, strings of characters, sounds, pictures) by a sequence of electronic pulses of fixed duration. Digital representation is preferred because it is less vulnerable to noise (signal disturbance), easy to compress, and easy to encrypt, preventing unauthorized capture of the information. Apart from its use in computing, digital technology is used by all major mobile communications networks, offering greater coverage, more reliable call handling, greater security and increased services compared with the previous analogue networks. >> analog; bit

Digital Enhanced Cordless Telecommunications (DECT) A European standard for cordless telephones that operate over a short distance from a fixed base station which is normally in the same room or building. Both voice and multimedia data can be transmitted, and the standard has been designed to allow interfacing with ISDN and GSM (Global System for Mobile Communication) networks. >>

Global System for Mobile Communication; Integrated Services Digital Network

digital media The use of digital recording to store media on computers and allow them to be processed by computer software. Different standards have been developed for the compression and storage of images, audio recordings and video recordings. **GIF** (**Graphics Interchange Format**) is a standard for the storage of still images, limited to 256 colours. **JPEG** (**Joint Photographic Experts Group**) is a standard for the compression and storage of continuous tone still images. **PNG** ('ping' – Portable Network Graphics) is a more recent (since 1995) graphics standard, with virtually unlimited colours and other advanced properties, which is a likely replacement for GIF. **MIDI** (**Musical Instrument Digital Interface**) is a format for representing the output from musical instruments which can be processed by a MIDI synthesizer, whether a computer or a sound-reproduction system. **MPEG** (**Motion Picture Experts Group**) is a standard for compressing video (including audio) sequences: **MPEG-1** is used for the storage of movies on CD-ROM; **MPEG-2** is for long-distance video transmission over digital communication lines. **WAV** (**Windows Waveform**) is a format for recording sound digitally. **MIME** (**Multipurpose Internet Mail Extension**) is a protocol for sending image, audio and video sequences across the Internet; it can handle images in GIF and JPEG formats, and video in MPEG format.

discussion list >> chatgroup

divert >> call divert

DNS >> domain name system

document description language (DDL) A methodology which enables documents to be handled in a consistent way when being electronically processed, through the use of special codes (*tags*). The first widely used system, **HTML (HyperText Markup Language)**, made use of tags indicating which kind of document element (e.g. main heading, subheading, figure caption, ordinary paragraph, item in a list) a particular section of text happens to be. A browser uses the tags in order to decide how to present the document to the user. **HTTP (HyperText Transfer Protocol)** is a protocol for locating documents stored on the Web and transferring the documents over the Internet from the Web site to the browser. **XML (Extensible Markup Language)** is a development of HTML which allows much more varied elements (e.g. video sequences) to be built into Web documents for transfer over the Internet. >> browser; Extensible Markup Language; Hypertext Markup Language; Internet; protocol; tags; Web

Document Type Description (DTD) >> **tags**

domain name system (DNS) The system which enables recognizable names (such as *bbc.co.uk*) to be associated with Internet locations (Internet Protocol numbers) that serve as routing addresses on the Internet. It is a directory organized in a hierarchy of levels, with each level separated by a dot. See the list on p. 177. >> second-level domain; top-level domain

dot In Web addresses, the character which separates the different types of name in the domain name hierarchy. >> domain name system; slash; Web

down A term describing a computer or piece of associated equipment which is not functioning, for whatever reason.
ORIGINAL USE
(as an adjective) *I can't send you anything at the moment; the server's down.*
NEW USE
(as an adjective, of any machine) out of action, unable to function
My bike's down; it needs a new set of brake pads.

download To transfer information from one kind of electronic storage to another, especially from a larger store to a smaller one, such as a file from a network to a personal computer; also, the information so transferred. >> network
ORIGINAL USE
(as a verb) *You can download the new version right now, and it's free!*
(as a noun) *That game is one of the best downloads I've had in ages.*
NEW USE
(as a verb) receive all the news, absorb information
It'll take me a while to download everything you've said.
(as a verb) tell all the news, send information, sound off
It's my turn to download now. (= I've heard all your gossip, now you listen to mine)
Note: some people object to this second usage, preferring to use *upload* for 'sending' and *download* for 'receiving'.
(as a noun) full report, complete briefing
Give me a download on what's going on in Paris.
(as a noun) harangue, sounding off
All I said was 'cigarette' and I got a right download about smoking.

draft folder An email facility which allows the user to store a message which is not in its final form. >> email

DTD >> tags

DTMF >> Dual Tone Multi Frequency

dual band A term describing mobile phones and networks that can operate in the two GSM (Global System for Mobile Communication) frequency bands of 900 Mhz and 1800 Mhz with seamless handover between the two. >> band; Global System for Mobile Communication

dual mode In mobile communications, a term describing a device capable of operating in digital and analog modes. >> analog; digital

Dual Tone Multi Frequency (DTMF) In mobile communications, the signal that is sent when a telephone keypad is pressed. Each digit is represented by two tones, one at a high frequency, the other at a low frequency. The system was designed to reduce errors when the telephone company was identifying which number had been dialled, and is now also used by others such as banks and credit-card companies when a user keys in a code number during a telephone transaction. Some mobile phones have a facility to turn off DTMF when the keypad is being used to note down numbers during a conversation. >> mobile phone

dump core >> coredump

duplex In mobile communications, a term describing a system in which data can be transferred between two devices in both directions. A **full-duplex** device can transmit and receive simultaneously, and therefore requires two data channels, whereas a **half-duplex** device either transmits or receives at any one time over a single channel. >> mobile communications

E

e- The standard prefix expressing electronic identity, now used
in hundreds of expressions such as *e-mail*, *e-cards* and *e-
cash*. The more widely used the word, the more likely it is
to drop the hyphen, as in *email*.

east >> **north/south/east/west**

e-commerce or **electronic commerce** The trend, in business and
administration, to use data communications to link their
computer systems directly to those of their suppliers and
customers. This allows many transactions to take place
without any human involvement, particularly the order-
ing of materials from suppliers on a just-in-time basis. The
term is increasingly used for the marketing of goods and
services directly to individual customers through the Internet. Because of the value of the commercial transactions taking place, there is now a great deal of emphasis
on making data communications highly secure, using
sophisticated techniques for encryption and authentication. >> Internet

e-conference >> **chatgroup**

EDGE >> **Enhanced Data rates for GSM Evolution**

editor >> **moderator**

EFR >> **Enhanced Full Rate**

EIR >> **International Mobile Equipment Identifier**

electronic commerce >> **e-commerce**

electronic discourse A name sometimes given to the kind of language used in computer-mediated communication, especially as found in dialogue situations such as email and chatgroups. >> chatgroup; email

electronic mail >> email/e-mail

electronic serial number (ESN) The unique 32-bit identification number embedded in a wireless phone by the manufacturer for use on an AMPS network. The number contains the manufacturer's identity code as well as the serial number of the device. Each time a call is placed, the ESN is automatically transmitted to the base station so that the wireless carrier's mobile switching office can check the call's validity. >> Advanced Mobile Phone System; International Mobile Equipment Identifier

email/e-mail or **electronic mail** The use of computer systems to transfer messages between individual users. Messages are usually stored centrally until acknowledged by the recipient. Email facilities are provided by most large computer systems for their users, and are also available on a national and international basis. >> instant message

emote In some virtual-world programs, a command which allows a participant to express a character's actions, feelings, gestures, facial expressions and so on; in some systems, called a **pose**. Emotes are typically statements with the verb in the third-person-singular present tense: a participant might type in *emote salute* for the character X, and this would appear on other participants' screens as 'X salutes'. >> character; emoticon; virtual world

emoticon or **smiley** A sequential combination of keyboard characters designed to convey the emotion associated with a particular facial expression. The simplest forms represent basic attitudes – positive, in the case of :) and negative in the case of : (. Emoticons are typed as a string on a single line, and usually located at the end of a sentence; most need to be read sideways. They are not very frequently used in emails, but a large number of jocular and artistically creative emoticons have been devised (see p. 117).

EMS >> smart messaging

encryption The process of scrambling a message to prevent it from being read by unauthorized parties. In digital systems the data is encoded with the aid of a key, a large binary number which is mathematically combined with the data using a special algorithm. The same key number is used at the receiving end to decode the message and restore the data to its original form. >> binary code; digital

Enhanced Data rates for GSM Evolution (EDGE) In mobile communications, a development in Global System for Mobile Communication technology that is intended to bring some 3G functionality to existing 2G networks by offering data transmission speeds up to 384 Kbps. >> generation; Global System for Mobile Communication; Kbps

Enhanced Full Rate (EFR) In mobile communications, a development in Global System for Mobile Communication technology that offers improved speech quality with less interference. Both the phone and the network must be suitably equipped. >> Global System for Mobile Communication; network

enhanced messaging service >> smart messaging

enterprise computing The provision of a uniform level of computing throughout an organization (or *enterprise*). An **enterprise network** is the network of connected workstations integrated throughout the organization, often linking many different sites. **Enterprise resource systems** are integrated computer systems which together provide support for the management of the main resources of an organization. >> network

EPOC In mobile communications, an open standard operating system for wireless information devices, developed in 1998 by Ericsson, Nokia, Matsushita (Panasonic), Motorola, Psion and Sony Ericsson in a joint venture called Symbian.

equipment identity register >> International Mobile Equipment Identifier

error message A screen message received from a computer program telling the user that a processing problem has taken place. The message might be generated by one's own computer, as with the all-too-familiar 'This program has performed an illegal operation and will be shut down', or come in from a network. >> 404 error

ESN >> electronic serial number

Ethernet A model of a Local Area Network in which the workstations of the network are linked by coaxial cable. If any network station wishes to communicate with another, it sends an addressed message along the cable; this is then recognized and picked up only by the workstation to which it is addressed. There is also a model of local area network, called a **'thin' ethernet,** which uses telephone wires but transmits data more slowly than in the standard **'thick' ethernet.** More recently, versions of Ethernet using unshielded twisted pair (UTP) cables linked to a central hub and operating at 100 Mbps have been developed. >> Local Area Network; Mbps; network

ETSI >> European Telecommunications Standards Institute

European Telecommunications Standards Institute (ETSI) A non-profit organization of manufacturers, network operators, service providers and other interested bodies which produces telecommunications standards that will be used throughout Europe and beyond. It is a European Union standards body, based in Sophia Antipolis, France. >> network; service provider

Extensible Markup Language (XML) The language developed by the World Wide Web Consortium as the universal format for structured documents and data on the Web. >> tags; Web; World Wide Web Consortium

eye candy The use of colours, photographs, animation and other graphical features to make a powerful onscreen visual effect. The concept is especially associated with the world of Internet commercial advertising, but screensaver displays are also sometimes described as eye candy.
ORIGINAL USE
(as a noun) *This site offers you more than just eye candy.*
NEW USE
(as a noun) something or someone eye-catching or externally attractive
Forget the eye candy; what's the engine like?

F

facemail A facetious coinage, based on *email*, for face-to-face communication. Such interaction would take place in **facetime**.

facetime >> **facemail**

FAQ or **frequently asked question** An optional facility provided by many Web sites, chatgroups and other computer-mediated operations, giving answers to a wide range of common enquiries. >> chatgroup; Web

favourite or **favorite** >> **bookmark**

FCC >> **Federal Communications Commission**

feature, it's a A catchphrase derived from the observation 'It's not a bug – it's a feature', referring to an unpalatable computer-using experience which the user is passing off lightly. The suggestion is that the program's displeasing behaviour is not an error, but a design-feature which the user has to get used to. The phrase will thus be encountered in any setting where machines (such as cars or washing-machines) do something unpleasant or unpredictable.

Federal Communications Commission (FCC) A federal body in the USA and its dependencies responsible for controlling communications by radio, television, wire, satellite and cable. >> Cellular Telecommunications and Internet Association

fifth-generation >> **generation**

firewall A technology which is used by organizations that have linked their enterprise computer systems into the Internet.

The firewall prevents users from outside the organization doing anything which would corrupt the system inside. One standard approach uses the firewall to filter out suspicious messages and discard them. Another approach offers a caller a copy of a system so that if the caller does anything that is malicious, this can be seen before the real system is damaged. >> enterprise computing; Internet

ORIGINAL USE

(as a noun) *Our firewall won't let me download that application.*

NEW USE

(as a noun) line of defence, barrier, shield

You've no chance with Emily. She's got a firewall you'll never get through.

firmware A permanent form of software built into a computer, essential for its basic operation. The term derives from the way the software has been made 'firm' by being burned into ROM chips. >> hardwired; ROM

ORIGINAL USE

(as a noun) *Read the installation notes of your firmware carefully before you upgrade.*

NEW USE

(as a noun) inherent quality, nature

A gin and tonic is an important part of Jim's firmware.

first-generation >> generation

flamage The aggressive content of an inflammatory electronic message (in an email or to a chatroom). >> flame

ORIGINAL USE

(as a noun) *I'm telling you – if you even mention strikes to Pete, you'll just get the usual flamage in return.*

NEW USE

(as a noun) any piece of inflammatory verbiage

All you'll get from him is a load of incoherent flamage.
If you go to the meeting, you'll hear all kinds of flamage about the government and the unions.

flame An aggressive, inflammatory, or hostile electronic message sent in an email or to a chatroom (also called **flaming**); also, the act of sending such a message. Flaming is always aggressive, related to a specific topic, and directed at an individual recipient (and therefore contrasts with spamming, which is often ludic or emotionally neutral, unspecific in content, and aimed at numbers of people). >> email; chatgroup; metaflaming; spam

ORIGINAL USE
(as a noun) *Ignore that last message; it's just a flame.*
(as a verb) *I got fed up with that group, with people flaming each other all the time.*

NEW USE
(as a noun) any provocative or ranting remark
Flames like that just don't bother me.
(as a verb) harangue, abuse, rant
When I bumped into Ted, he started to flame me for no reason at all.
(as a verb) talk boringly and at length about a subject, especially in an aggressive way
I'm fed up with you flaming about the trains; let's change the subject.

RELATED USE
flame on, talk angrily at length, especially in an aggressive way
What do you keep flaming on at me for!

flamebait, flame-bait An electronic message sent to a site with the intention of triggering an angry response. >> flame; flame war.

ORIGINAL USE

Ignore that last message about Star Trek *being boring – it's just flamebait.*

NEW USE

(as a noun) a provocative remark intended to trigger an angry response

That's the most obvious bit of flamebait I've heard in a long time.

flamer Someone who sends an aggressive or inflammatory electronic message (in an email or to a chatroom), especially someone who does this habitually or for fun. >> flame

ORIGINAL USE

(as a noun) *Flamers are not welcome at this site.*

NEW USE

(as a noun) someone who is deliberately provocative or argumentative

You're a real flamer, aren't you? Always stirring things up!

flame war, flame-war An angry electronic dispute in a public forum (as in a chatroom). >> flame; flamebait

ORIGINAL USE

(as a noun) *There's a flame war going on in that newsgroup about fishing rights.*

NEW USE

(as a noun) any acrimonious dispute

Sales have started a real flame war with Accounts; it's getting very personal.

flaming An aggressive or inflammatory electronic message (in an email or to a chatroom); also, the act of sending such messages.

ORIGINAL USE

(as a noun) *Flaming is one of the curses of the Internet.*

NEW USE
(as a noun) the use of deliberately aggressive language in a spoken exchange
Just listen to all that flaming going on.

flush To abort an output operation from a computer; also, to delete an unwanted entity from a file or program.
ORIGINAL USE
(as a verb) *We'll have to flush that print-run – we're using the wrong paper.*
NEW USE
(as an intransitive verb) leave, finish [doing something]
It's nearly seven o'clock – time to flush. (= go home)
(as a transitive verb) ignore or exclude someone
If Joe keeps on asking for a loan, he'll end up with everybody flushing him.

FOMA (Freedom of Mobile Multimedia Access) A full 3G development of an I-Mode system launched in 2001 by NTT DoCoMo, Japan, utilizing broadband technology. Users are able to send or receive data at the same time as holding a voice conversation. >> broadband; generation; I-Mode

four-oh-four, 404 A term identifying an error message shown on screen when a browser makes a faulty request to a server (typically because a page or site no longer exists). The expression derives from the 'file not found' message sent out as a response to a faulty enquiry by staff in Room 404 at CERN, Switzerland, where the Web was devised. >> browser; error message; server; Web
ORIGINAL USE
(as an adjective) *I've got one of those 404 error messages onscreen again.*
NEW USE

(as an adjective, applied to humans) confused, blank, uncertain

You've got a 404 look on your face.

(as an adjective) stupid, uninformed, clueless

Don't bother trying to get an answer out of that 404 headcase.

(as an adjective) unavailable, not around

Sorry, Mike's 404. (= not in his room, and I don't know where)

(as a verb) make no progress

Looks like Mike's 404-ing. (= not getting anywhere)

fourth-generation >> generation

framing An email process in which the receiver responds to individual points within the body of the sender's message, rather than replying to the whole message at the beginning or end. Typographical conventions, using pipes (|) or angle brackets (>) at the beginning of lines, or varying colours, demarcate the alternating pieces of text. >> email

fried Descriptive of a serious hardware failure, especially one due to an electrical malfunction (and thus displaying physical signs of burning).

ORIGINAL USE

(as an adjective) *We must have had a power surge, or something – the mother-board's fried.*

NEW USE

(as an adjective, applied to humans) overworked, worn out

My brain is totally fried after that long session.

front end A computer which carries out an initial range of elementary tasks on behalf of another, more powerful

computer; also, a piece of software which provides an interface with a more complex program behind it.
ORIGINAL USE
(as a noun) *We have a new application which provides a good front end for our print management system.*
NEW USE
(as a noun, applied to humans) mode of behaviour where someone is talking without paying attention
If I can get past your front end, I'll bring you up to date.

full-duplex >> duplex

functionality The range of operations which a computer or program allows its user to perform.

G

G >> generation

gag In virtual-world environments, a sanction imposed by one player (P) on another (Q) whose behaviour has been deemed unacceptable, enabling Q's messages to be invisible on P's screen; also, the act of imposing such a sanction. An accumulation of gag decisions by several players would soon convey the group's antipathy, inculcating in Q a sense of communicative isolation. >> newt; toad; virtual world

gateway A facility provided between computer networks to enable a network operating according to one protocol to pass messages to a second network using a different protocol. >> network; protocol; WAP gateway

Gb >> gigabyte

geek Someone who is technically knowledgeable about computers and the Internet; also, anyone who spends a significant proportion of social (as opposed to professional) life online. Geeks tend to be younger, digitally aware people; they are distinguished from **geezers,** who are older people used to working within an analogue frame of reference. Within the computing world the noun has a positive connotation, as does the verb: to spend time using computers for work or socializing. Outside this world, the terms have attracted some negative overtones, as has 'nerd', with which there is some overlap in usage. >> alpha geek; analog; nerd

ORIGINAL USE
(as a noun) *The geeks at Microworld have come up with another great idea.*
(as a verb) *I plan to geek all Saturday with buddies in California.*

NEW USE
waste time by always being online
(as a verb) *I really must stop geeking every weekend and go out and get a life.*

RELATED USE
geek out, start using computer jargon in a non-specialist situation
I can't explain the problems we've been having without geeking out.

geezer >> geek

General Packet Radio System (GPRS) An extension to the non-voice services of a mobile-phone network which breaks data up into a number of packets prior to transmission and reassembles them at the receiving end. The process is similar to that used by the Internet, and brings Internet access to mobile phones. By making more efficient use of the network radio resources, more users can operate at the same time, and transmission speeds are also increased. >> Internet; mobile phone; network

generation (G) A significant stage of development within computing and mobile communications technology. In computing, **first-generation** computers were the early devices in the 1940s and 1950s, built using thermionic valves. **Second-generation** computers replaced these valves by discrete transistors. **Third-generation** computers replaced transistors by integrated circuits. **Fourth-generation** computers were built with very large-scale integrated circuits (VLSI). **Fifth-generation** computers are those showing artificial intelligence with which we can communicate in natural language. With mobile phones, 2G is the name for the technology currently deployed by most GSM (Global System for Mobile Communication) network operators. 3G is the emerging technology specified by IMT-2000. Some current developments that are an intermediate stage on the way to full 3G implementation are referred to as 2.5G. >> EDGE; Global System for Mobile Communication; IMT-2000

generic code >> top-level domain

Ghz >> hertz

GIF >> digital media

gig >> gigabyte

gigabyte One thousand million bytes (actually 1024 x 1024 x 1024); abbreviated in writing as **Gb** and in colloquial speech as **gig**. >> byte

glitch A sudden interruption in the functioning of a computer program which interferes with its normal usage.

ORIGINAL USE

(as a noun) *There's some sort of glitch causing my keyboard to freeze.*

NEW USE

(as a noun, applied to humans) unexpected problem, sudden irregularity

We got as far as Birmingham, then there was a glitch – a bus never turned up on time.

(as a verb) make an error of judgement, behave wrongly

Mike glitched badly by not sending the letters out first class.

Global Positioning System (GPS) A means of determining an exact position on the Earth, using a system of satellites and an appropriate receiver. Twenty-four satellites make up the American NAVSTAR system, orbiting about 20,000 km above the Earth. The **Standard Positioning Service (SPS)** is accurate to about 100 m (325 ft) and the **Precise Positioning Service (PPS)** is accurate to 22 m (70 ft). The **Differential GPS (DGPS)** also uses additional fixed stations on Earth and gives horizontal position accuracy to about 3 m (10 ft). >> location service; wireless

Global System for Mobile Communication (GSM) A standardization group set up in 1982 to define a common standard for mobile communications in Europe. The first commercial system began operating in 1991, and the standard has now become worldwide. GSM exists in three different versions: GSM 900 and GSM 1800 are used in Europe and Asia, and GSM 1900 is used in North America. Mobile-phone handsets are available which will work on all three bands (**tri-band** handsets). >> hertz; mobile phone

god >> wizard

GPRS >> General Packet Radio System

GPS >> Global Positioning System

Graphics Interchange Format >> digital media

graphic user interface (GUI) In computing, an operating
  system or environment that displays options on the screen
  as graphical symbols, icons, or photographs.

gronked Term describing a computer which has crashed or
  broken down.
  ORIGINAL USE
  (as an adjective) *The scanner was gronked, so we had to
  retype the page.*
  NEW USE
  (as an adjective, applied to humans) exhausted, very tired;
  unwell
  I feel totally gronked after all that discussion.
  RELATED USE
  gronk out, stop being active
  *I've been here all day, without a break, so I'm gronking
  out.*

GSM >> Global System for Mobile Communication

guest A visitor to a virtual-world environment. >> virtual
  world; wizard

GUI >> graphic user interface

H

hack To gain unauthorized access to a computer site or file; also, the computing solution which enables someone to do this. >> hacker; phishing

ORIGINAL USE

(as a verb) *It should only take me a few minutes to hack that site.*

also, **hack into**

I've managed to hack into their confidential list of clients.
(as a noun) *I've found an excellent hack which lets you get at a whole range of software.*
(as an adjective) *This piece of software protects you from hack attacks.*

NEW USE

(as a verb, of any problem) solve, crack, work out
I've hacked it: there wasn't a fuse in the plug.
(as a noun) clever idea which solves a problem, helpful technical trick
That was a good hack, thinking to phone John at his girlfriend's.

hacker A computer expert who enjoys communicating with other remote computers, usually via the telephone network or the Internet, to explore their properties or content. The usual implication is that the task is sufficiently difficult to act as a challenge. In recent years, the term has acquired a pejorative sense, referring to those who access remote computers without permission, often obtaining access to confidential information of a personal or business nature. This usage is deprecated by true hackers, who refer to such people as **crackers**. Malicious hacking is now illegal within several countries. >> Internet; phreaker; spoof (2); virus half-duplex >> duplex

handheld computer >> personal digital assistant

Handheld Device Markup Language (HDML) A proprietary
language for defining hypertext-like content for handheld
computers, mobile phones and other devices with small
screens. It was developed by Unwired Planet (now Open-
wave.com), and produced before the WAP standard was
released. >> Hypertext Markup Language; Wireless Application Protocol

hand off The process of automatically transferring a mobile-
phone call from one cell site to another as the user moves
through a service area. >> cell

handshaking The initial set of operations which two computers must go through when making contact with each
other, so that they work together smoothly. The procedure establishes such factors as the computer language
and protocols involved and the rate at which data can be
processed. >> protocol
ORIGINAL USE
(as a noun) *Once handshaking is finished, all messages
start with a special symbol.*
(as an adjective) *Be careful, as this procedure will alter the
handshaking operation protocols.*
(as a verb) *The two modems don't take long to handshake.*
NEW USE
(as a noun) mutual feedback while talking (e.g. head-
nodding, smiling)
*Jim and Joan seem to be getting on fine, judging by the
handshaking.*

hardwired, hard-wired Term describing a circuit using a direct physical connection which performs a specific and unchangeable function. When applied to the information content within a computer, it implies that the data cannot be removed or overwritten. >> firmware; wired
ORIGINAL USE
(as an adjective) *The system is completely hardwired, which eliminates the possibility of interference.*
NEW USE
(as an adjective, applied to humans, especially the brain) built in, part of nature
[magazine heading] *Are human beings hard-wired for war?*

hash A common name for the # keyboard symbol, also referred to by a variety of colloquialisms, such as *sharp*, *crunch* and *cross-hatch*. >> punctuation

HDML >> **Handheld Device Markup Language**

header or **heading** The preformatted upper area of an email message, typically consisting of the addresses of receiver and sender, a topic description, and an indication of the date and time sent. Other header areas have been designed to accommodate file attachments, status indications (such as whether a message is urgent), and addresses which are to receive copies of a message. >> attachment; Cc; email

hertz (Hz) The standard unit of frequency; named after German physicist Heinrich Hertz (1857–94). Defined as the number of complete cycles per second, it is applicable to all wave and periodic phenomena. Wireless communications use frequencies measured in multiples of one million hertz, or **megahertz (Mhz)**, particularly 800 Mhz, 900

Mhz, 1800 Mhz, and 1900 Mhz; the latter frequencies are also measured in thousand-million units or **gigahertz** (**Ghz**) – 18 Ghz, 19 Ghz.

holding >> call holding

host (**1**) A computer in a network that provides a service or passes on data to other computers. Over 170 million host computers were connected to the Internet by the year 2004. >> Internet

host (**2**) **>> moderator**

hotlink >> hypertext link

hotlist A personally compiled list of Internet addresses which are of particular interest or relevance to the user.
ORIGINAL USE
(as a noun) *I've got a great hotlist of endangered animal sites now.*
NEW USE
(as a noun) list of special people, places, etc.
I've invited Chris; she's been on my hotlist for ages.

hotspot (**1**) An area on a screen which can be activated by a mouse click or similar stimulus. In a Web page, it is a location (such as a word, an address, or an image) which contains a link (a **hotlink**) to some other page. >> hyperlink; Web (**2**) **>> wireless**

HTML >> document description language; Hypertext Mark-up Language

HTTP >> document description language; Web

hyper- A prefix designating an entity, event, or other phenomenon which relates to the ability of the Web to make electronic links (*hyperlinks*) between and within sites and pages. Hundreds of coinages have emerged since the early 1990s, such as *hyperfiction* and *hyperzine*. >> Hypertext Markup Language; Web

hyperlink >> **hypertext link**

hypermedia All types of document which can be held on a computer, consisting of elements of text, audio and video sequences, and computer programs, linked together in such a way that users can move from one element to another and back again. The computer programs can be activated from within the document and may modify the document. When these operations are carried out within a database consisting solely of texts, the domain is known as *hypertext*. >> hypertext; Hypertext Markup Language

hypertext A computer document containing cross-references which can be activated (by clicking a mouse) to transfer the reader to another part of the document or to another document. >> hypermedia; hypertext link; Hypertext Markup Language
ORIGINAL USE
(as a noun) *As a piece of hypertext this page isn't so good because it has hardly any links.*
NEW USE
(as a noun) hidden world, alternative dimension
He's living in hypertext. (= he's got a lot to hide)

hypertext link or **hyperlink**, also **hotlink** The electronic jump that a user can make in moving from one Web page or site to another. It is the most fundamental structural property of the Web. >> dead link; hypermedia; link rot; Web

Hypertext Markup Language (HTML) A method of marking a document so that it can be displayed as a Web page. The language, derived from **SGML (Standard Generalized Markup Language)** by early Internet developers, was defined by an Internet Engineering Task Force working group. The layout and presentation of a document on the screen, and the ability to link to other documents, are controlled by embedded tags which are hidden from view when the document is viewed in a Web browser. HTML is slowly being replaced by **XHTML,** which is a combination of XML and HTML. >> Extensible Markup Language; hypertext; markup language; tags; Web

HyperText Transfer Protocol >> document description language; Web

Hz >> hertz

icon A small picture on a computer screen which can initiate a computational process when activated (usually by placing the cursor on it and clicking the mouse-key).

ID >> caller ID

idling The practice of a normally active member of a chatgroup to stay connected while not making a contribution to the group. The reasons include having one's attention taken up by some other task or simply not having anything to say. Idling should not be confused with *lurking*, where there is a deliberate attempt to hide one's presence. >> chatgroup; lurking

IEGMP >> Independent Expert Group on Mobile Phones (IEGMP)

IM >> instant message

IMEI >> International Mobile Equipment Identifier

I-Mode A packet-based system that enables a mobile phone to function as a Web browser, launched in 1999 by the Japanese mobile operator NTT DoCoMo, with over 40 million subscribers by the end of 2003. Transmission speed is 9600 bps for standard handsets, but up to 384 Kbps for FOMA equipment. >> bps; broadband; browser; FOMA; Web

imp, implementer >> wizard

IMT-2000 A framework or group of standards defined by the International Telecommunication Union which will enable a subscriber to access mobile-phone networks anytime anywhere without the need for pre-arranged roaming agreements between the home and visiting networks. It will also deliver broadband multimedia content at high speed. >> broadband; International Telecommunication Union; Universal Mobile Telecommunications System

inbox The location in an email facility to which incoming messages are sent. >> email

incaps >> bicapitalization

incoming call alert A mobile-phone function which tells the user that a new call is being received. A set of options is available from which the user can choose. >> mobile phone

Independent Expert Group on Mobile Phones (IEGMP) A group of medical and technical experts set up in 1999 by the British Government to investigate potential health hazards arising from the use of mobile phones. Their report, making various recommendations about the use of mobile phones and the siting of base stations, was published in 2000. >> mobile phone

information superhighway >> **cyberspace**

Infrared Data Association (IrDA) An association of major companies that develops standards for wireless data transmission between computers using infrared radiation, similar to the common TV remote control. The system requires line-of-sight alignment of the IrDA ports of the two devices exchanging data.

instant message (IM) An email which informs the recipient the moment it arrives at a computer (instead of being left in an inbox to be discovered later). The application which enables this to happen is an **instant messenger**. >> email

Integrated Services Digital Network (ISDN) A service provided by the Posts, Telegraph and Telephones Authorities, which allows voice and data communications to be effected on the same line. This enables voice messaging to be carried out in the same way as data transmission. Facilities are available also for transmitting television pictures of medium quality. >> Public Switch Telephone Network

interactive paging >> **two-way paging**

intercaps >> **bicapitalization**

interface An apparatus designed to connect any two scientific instruments so that they can be operated jointly; also, the apparatus which enables a user to interact with an instrument, such as a computer or mobile phone.

International Mobile Equipment Identifier (IMEI) A 15-digit number that uniquely identifies a mobile phone in a GSM (Global System for Mobile Communication) network; it is made up of a 6-digit-type approval code, a 2-digit manufacturer identity code, a 6-digit serial number, and a spare digit. The number is transmitted when the phone is switched on, and the number can be checked against the equipment identity register (EIR) at the network and switching subsystem (NSS) to ensure it is an authorized unit. >> electronic serial number; Global System for Mobile Communication; network and switching subsystem

International Packet Switching Service (IPSS) A service provided by the Posts, Telegraph and Telephones Authorities which allows a computer to send a packet of data to another computer anywhere in the world, without a dedicated physical wire communication being established between the two. The sender is charged only for the number of packets and their destination, and not for the length of time that the sender and receiver are linked together. >> packet switching

International Telecommunication Union (ITU) An agency of the United Nations, which since 1947 has promoted worldwide co-operation in all aspects of telecommunications, such as the regulation of global telecom networks and radio frequencies. Its headquarters is in Geneva, Switzerland.

Internet or **Net** (sometimes not capitalized) An association of computer networks with common standards which enable messages to be sent from any host on one network to any host on any other. It developed in the 1970s in the USA as an experimental network designed to support military research, and steadily grew to include federal, regional, campus and other users. It is now the world's largest computer network, with over 170 million hosts connected by 2004, providing an increasing range of services and enabling unprecedented numbers of people to be in touch with each other through email, chatgroups and the provision of digital 'pages' on every conceivable topic. The *World Wide Web* is an Internet facility designed for multimedia use, in which individuals or organizations make available 'pages' of information to other users anywhere in the world, generally at no cost, but in the case of certain commercial operations (such as an encyclopaedia or electronic journal) through subscription. During the 1990s, alongside claims that the Internet provided fresh opportunities for self-publishing, creativity and freedom of speech, there was increasing concern about the safeguarding of rights of privacy and intellectual property (copyright), the application of existing laws to the Internet (in such domains as pornography and libel), the extent to which the content of some of the new 'virtual communities' can or should be regulated, and the impact that the growing numbers of Internet communities ('cyburbia') will have on individuals and on society as a whole. The potential of the Internet is also currently limited by relatively slow data-transmission speeds, and by the problems of information management and retrieval posed by the existence of such a vast amount of information. >> broadband; chat; email; host; Internet Corporation for Assigned Names and Numbers; Internet Protocol; Internet Society; Net-; network; WAP; Web

Internet Corporation for Assigned Names and Numbers (ICANN) The international body which has the responsibility for regulating the addresses, names and numbers that form the interactive structure of the Internet. It is a non-profit corporation, formed in 1998, which took over the functions of a number of loosely related bodies which had grown up as the Internet evolved. ICANN was established as a result of the growing international and commercial importance of the Internet, which required the creation of a more formalized, transparent, accountable and globally representative organization. >> domain name system; Internet

Internet Protocol (IP) The communications protocol which underlies the Internet, allowing large computer networks all over the world to communicate with each other efficiently. An **Internet Protocol Address** is the numerical address which identifies an Internet location to member computers. Human users usually rely on the textual names made available through the domain name system. >> domain name system; Internet; protocol

Internet ready A term describing a computer or mobile-phone handset that is suitably programmed for Internet access. >> Internet; mobile phone

Internet Relay Chat (IRC) A real-time international chatgroup system which allows users to be simultaneously in touch with each other by joining a channel (or chatroom) on a network. Each channel is devoted to a particular topic, the identifier being a word or abbreviation prefixed by a hash symbol, such as *#sport*, *#gb* (= Great Britain). >> chatgroup

Internet Service Provider (ISP) A company providing Internet access to users, whether organizations or individuals. >> Internet; service provider

Internet Society (ISOC) An international organization for global co-operation and co-ordination for the technologies and applications which comprise the Internet. >> Internet

intranet A private computer network within an organization. The term is not usually capitalized (unlike *Internet*), because there are millions of intranets around the world. >> Internet

IP >> **Internet Protocol**

IPSS >> **International Packet Switching Service**

IRC >> **Internet Relay Chat**

IrDA >> **Infrared Data Association**

ISDN >> **Integrated Services Digital Network**

ISOC >> **Internet Society**

ISP >> **Internet Service Provider**

itemized billing A complete list of all calls made from a subscriber's mobile phone. >> mobile phone

ITU >> **International Telecommunication**

J

JANET >> Joint Academic Network

Joint Academic Network (JANET) A computer network provided in the UK to link computer centres in higher education and research establishments, providing electronic mail, file transfer and the ability for a user at one computer centre to log into the facilities at another. A particular use of JANET allows researchers at many universities to scan the library catalogues of other universities in order to locate books. Gateways are provided from JANET to BITNET, Internet, and USENET. >> Internet

Joint Photographic Experts Group >> digital media

JPEG >> digital media

K

Kb >> kilobyte

Kbps An abbreviation for **kilobits per second,** referring to the rate of data transmission, where a kilobit = 1012 bits. >> bps

keyguard >> keypad lock

keypad The set of alphanumeric push buttons on a mobile phone. >> alphanumeric; keypad lock

keypad lock A mobile-phone function which disables the push buttons on a handset, thus preventing calls being made accidentally. >> keypad

keypad tones The sounds made when the push buttons on a mobile-phone handset are pressed. >> keypad; mobile phone

kilobyte One thousand bytes (actually 1024); abbreviated as **Kb**. >> byte

L

lag The gap between the time of posting a message and the time at which it reaches the recipient's computer. Many messages are received virtually instantaneously, but problems of bandwidth processing, traffic density and other factors can introduce delays which can last from a few seconds to several hours or even days. >> bandwidth; post

LAN >> Local Area Network

LCD >> liquid crystal display

link >> hypertext link

link rot A process of deteriorating hypertext linkage at a Web site, due to the site owner removing pages or altering page-names without telling anyone. >> hypertext link; Web

liquid crystal display (LCD) A display that uses the variable light-deflecting properties of liquid crystals. Liquid crystals are organic materials, crystalline in the solid state, which form a partially ordered state (the **liquid crystal state**) upon melting, and become true liquids only after the temperature is raised further. Their optical transparency can be reduced by applying electric fields – a property extensively exploited in displays for watches, calculators, mobile phones, portable computers and other electronic devices.

list-owner >> moderator

LISTSERV A software system for managing electronic mailing lists. (The lack of a final -*e* in the name reflects the eight-character name-processing limitation of computers at the time it was devised, in 1986.) >> mailing list

LMDS >> Local Multipoint Distribution System

Local Area Network (LAN) A system which allows communication between computers situated within a well-defined geographical area, and which does not use the public-telephone system. By contrast, a **Wide Area Network** or **Long Distance Network** allows computer communication over a large geographical area, generally using the telephone system. >> Ethernet; network

Local Multipoint Distribution System. (LMDS) A microwave radio system employing small cells of 3–10 miles diameter, operating in the 10–40 Ghz band, providing broadband service to many users from a single base station. One application of the service is the provision of high-quality interactive multimedia content from Web sites. >> cell; Web

location services A marriage of the location-identifying technology from GPS with mobile-phone technology to provide selected Internet content (particularly advertisements) to a user, as determined by the user's location. >> Global Positioning System; Internet; mobile phone

lock code >> Personal Identification Number

log or **archive** The store of messages which has been sent to a chatgroup, indexed and catalogued (with varying level of detail among the different systems) in terms of date, topic, author, etc. The term is also used more generally in computing for an electronic record of events in the order in which they happened. >> chatgroup; thread

log on To carry out the sequence of operations which enables someone to access a computer or computer network; also **log in**, especially when a password is required. People may 'log in' or 'log someone in' (as when a user wants to give someone else access to a database). The opposite process, whereby access is terminated, is to **log off** or **log out** (or 'log someone out'). One may also **log on to** a computer system and **log out of** it. Corresponding noun uses refer to the procedure itself: **a log-in/login** or **log-out/logout**. Adjectival use can be seen in such references as 'log-on operation' and 'log-out time'. >> network
ORIGINAL USE
(as a verb) *It'll only take me a moment to log on to the site.*
NEW USE
(as a verb) join in, take part in
I'm going to log in to Dick's party on the way home.
also, **log on**
RELATED USE
log off (as a verb) leave, take oneself off
Time for me to log off, guys, I'm getting tired.
also, **log out**

Long Distance Network >> Local Area Network

lose, sometimes **loss** The unexpected inability of a computer program to cope with a required task. >> -age

ORIGINAL USE
(as a noun) *It's been an awful day trying to get those pictures scanned – one lose after another.*
NEW USE
(as a noun, applied to humans) unco-operative person, unpleasant individual
John's a real lose when it comes to buying a round.
(as a noun, applied to things) failure, unsuccessful attempt to make something work
I wouldn't put in that sort of oil – that's bound to be a lose.
RELATED USE
win (as a noun) success, achievement
They've both managed to get tickets. What a win!

loss >> lose

LPMUD >> MUD

lurk >> lurking

lurker >> lurking

lurking The practice of visiting a chatgroup environment and reading the messages it contains, but deliberately not wanting to make any contribution to the discussion, or even wanting one's presence to be known; people who do this are called **lurkers**; the activity is to **lurk**. The motives include a newcomer reluctance to be involved, academic curiosity (researching some aspect of Internet culture) and voyeurism. >> chatgroup; idling

M

mailbomb The sending of many messages to a server in an attempt to shut it down, or to an individual's e-address;

also, to send such messages. The reasons can include anything from personal grievance to an orchestrated political campaign. **Anti-mailbomb** programs have been devised in an attempt to counter such measures. >> email; server

mailing list An Internet site containing a set of e-addresses to which owners can send messages. All messages sent to the site will be automatically redirected to all members on the list. A list is often monitored by a moderator. >> chatgroup; moderator

maintainer >> moderator

MAN >> Metropolitan Area Network

markup language A means of coding documents so that they can be stored in a document database in a standard way and presented on an output medium in the correct form for that medium. >> Extensible Markup Language; Hypertext Markup Language

Mb >> megabyte

Mbps An abbreviation for **megabits per second,** referring to the rate of data transmission, where megabit = 1024 x 1024 bits. >> bps

M-commerce or **mobile commerce, mobile e-commerce** The use of mobile phones to buy and sell goods over the Internet. >> Internet; mobile phone

meg >> megabyte

megabyte One million bytes (actually 1024 x 1024); abbreviated in writing as **Mb** and in colloquial speech as **meg.** >> byte

megahertz One million hertz; abbreviated as **Mhz**. >> hertz

memory A part of an electronic device which stores, either permanently or temporarily, programs and data. There are two basic types of internal memory used in digital devices: *Random Access Memory* (RAM) and *Read-Only Memory* (ROM). >> access time; RAM; ROM

menu In computing, a set of options presented to the user by a computer program. A program which communicates with the user solely by providing choices from interlinked menus is said to be **menu-driven**. The menu facility is used extensively, in addition to icons, in graphic user interfaces. In mobile communications, the term refers to the displayed list of options on a mobile phone, enabling the user to select a desired facility. >> graphic user interface; icon; mobile phone

ORIGINAL USE
(as a noun) *Press the return key and you'll get a menu with a list of options.*

NEW USE
(as a noun, applied to humans) routine, normal way of behaving
Sorry, working Saturdays isn't on my menu.

RELATED USE
(as an adjective, applied to humans) unoriginal, unable or unwilling to go beyond a norm
Fred would never dare do that – he's totally menu-driven.

message alert tone The distinctive tone sounded by a mobile phone when a new text message is received. The tone can be personalized by the user. >> Short Messaging Service

messaging The transfer of a text message from a mobile handset or personal digital assistant to one or more persons via email, Short Messaging Service, paging, or other method. >> chat, email; pager; personal digital assistant; Short Messaging Service

metaflaming An angry exchange in emails or in a chatroom about the topic of flaming – 'flaming about flaming'. It often takes the form of an argument in which one person accuses another of flaming, which the other emphatically denies. >> flame

Metropolitan Area Network (MAN) A computer network which serves an area roughly equal to a city or large town, and thus falls between a Local Area Network and a Wide Area Network. An example of a MAN is a cable TV network, which could be used also for two-way data transmission. >> network

Mhz >> **megahertz**

midcaps >> **bicapitalization**

MIDI >> **digital media**

MIME >> **digital media**

MMS >> **Multimedia Messaging Service**

mobile communications A system which provides a simple, convenient means of communication for people who wish to keep in touch when travelling. The first mobile communication system was ship-borne radio, and there have since been widespread developments in the field of military communications. In modern times the term also refers to personal communication systems such as CB radio, radio paging, and car and pocket phones which use cellular radio. Cellular radio employs local radio transmitters, covering small areas (*cells*), which receive and transmit calls in association with the telecommunications network. Direct-dial calls using special handsets were a major development of the 1990s. >> cell; mobile phone; pager

mobile phone or **mobile** (UK), **cellphone, cell phone** (US), also **cellular** A portable telephone handset, used with a cellular radio or other mobile communication system, small enough to fit into a pocket or bag. It enables users to make direct-dial telephone calls from any location within the service area of the network they have opted to use. Not all networks are cellular in the strict sense that they pass a signal from one local transmitteer (cell) to the next; a noncellular network transmits by sending a single signal out to the whole area it serves. >> cell; network; predictive text input; SIM card; wireless

modem An abbreviation of **MOdulator/DEModulator,** a device which converts digital information from computers into electrical signals that can be transmitted over the analogue telephone system and vice versa.

moderator A common designation for the manager of a chatgroup; other terms include **editor, host, postmaster, maintainer,** and **list-owner.** Other distinctions may be made within these terms: for example, the person who owns the list may not be the same as the person who maintains it. The role of a moderator varies between chat systems; some have only filtering powers (deciding whether a message should appear or not), others have editing powers, enabling them to shorten messages, remove offensive language, etc. >> chatgroup

MOO An acronym of **MUD Object Orientated,** a text-based database, creating a vivid imaginary environment where users interact in real time, and containing programmed objects (such as roads, furniture, weapons) that the participants can introduce and manipulate. Many types of MOO have been devised, the most frequented being *LambdaMOO.* Those who identify with MOOs as a separate genre from MUDs call themselves **MOOers** or **MOOsters.** A verb use is also available, as in 'I was mooing for hours'. >> MUD; virtual world

morf An abbreviation of **male or female,** often used in chatrooms as a query message when it is not clear which gender the sender is. Reasons for the ambiguity include the use of a gender-neutral name (such as *Chris*) or the use of a genderless nickname (such as *Boz*). There is of course no way of knowing whether the subsequent clarification is truthful. >> sorg

morph >> **character**

Motion Picture Experts Group >> **digital media**

MPEG >> **digital media**

MU* >> **MUD**

MUCK >> **MUD**

MUD An acronym for **Multi-User Dimension** (originally, **Multi-User Dungeon**), a text-based database which creates a vivid imaginary environment in which users interact in real time. Several kinds of MUD have been devised, using various programming languages which permit different kinds of activity to take place, such as **LPMUDs** (based on the LPC programming language) and **TinyMUDs** (so-called because its program was smaller than those used in previous MUDs). Related genres have been devised, with names deriving from the word 'mud', such as **MUCKs** and **MUSHes**. The whole domain is sometimes abbreviated as **MU*** (where the asterisk is the wildcard symbol). The subject-matter of MU*s can be inferred, with varying amounts of certainty, by examining the full name, such as *Dragon-MUCK* or *Lion King MUCK*. Participants refer to themselves as **MUDders** or **MUDsters**. A verb use is also available, as in 'I was mudding all night'. >> MOO; virtual world

MUD Object Orientated >> **MOO**

multimedia The tools and techniques used in computing to allow computer programs to handle text, sound, picture, animation and video components. >> streaming

Multimedia Messaging Service (MMS) Emerging 3G technology and standards to enable delivery of voice, text, graphics, audio and video to mobile phones. >> generation; mobile phone

Multipurpose Internet Mail Extension >> **digital media**

multitasking, multi-tasking The running of more than one program simultaneously on a computer.
ORIGINAL USE
(as a noun) *That operating system is really good at multitasking – it's really increased our output.*
NEW USE
(as a noun, applied to humans) carrying out of more than one activity at the same time

I'm just no good at multitasking, apart from when I'm eating and watching TV.
The office is going more and more in for multitasking now; I'm supposed to be on reception as well as answer the phone and keep an eye on the security screens.
(as a verb) carry out more than one activity at the same time
I don't mind you interrupting; I'm multitasking already.

Multi-User Dimension / Dungeon >> MUD

MUSH >> MUD

Musical Instrument Digital Interface >> digital media

mutter A command used in some virtual-world programs which enables a character to make a remark which is seen by all but one of the other participants. >> character; virtual world

nak >> ack

NAM >> Number Assignment Module

nano [probably from *nanosecond*, a thousand-millionth part of a second] A very short period of time (replacing traditional idioms such as *sec(ond)* and *mo(ment)*).
ORIGINAL USE
The transient currents flow for a very short time (of the order of ten nanoseconds).
NEW USE
(as a noun) *I'll be with you in a nano.*

NAVSTAR >> Global Positioning System

nerd Someone fascinated with technology in general, and often with the computer in particular (though less sharply focused on Internet matters than a 'geek' would be). The name has a strongly positive connotation within the computing community, but it often carries negative connotations in everyday speech, suggesting a person who is too narrowly focused, lacks social skills, or is excessively studious. >> geek

Net >> Internet

Net- A prefix designating an entity, event, or other phenomenon which relates to the Internet. Hundreds of coinages have emerged since the 1980s, including *netlag*, *netdead*, *netnews* and of course *Netspeak*. The term also has some use as a combining form, as in *hypernet*, *Usenet*, *JANET*, *EcoNet* and a host of organizational names. >> Internet; netiquette; netizen; Netlish; Netspeak; Netsplit

netiquette The conventions which govern acceptable behaviour when engaging in Internet dialogue, especially in emailing, chatrooms and virtual worlds. The politeness conventions vary greatly, and many sites now give guidance about such matters as greeting and leaving a group, addressing messages, the sort of subject-matter which is unacceptable, and the avoidance of offensive language. >> chatgroup; email; flame; troll; virtual world

netizen Someone who uses the Internet (or some other network) so often that they might be considered to be a 'citizen of the Internet'. It is one of several coinages based on the word *Net* describing people who join particular Net communities, such as chatgroups: they include **netties**, netters, and netheads. You know you are a real netizen when all of your friends have an @ in their names. >> chatgroup; Internet

Netlish or Weblish A name sometimes used for the kind of English found on the Internet. >> Internet

Netspeak or cyberspeak Terms used by some commentators, devised on analogy with such words as *doublespeak* (as in the work of George Orwell) and *airspeak* (for the language of air-traffic control), to describe the kind of distinctive language found on the Internet. >> Internet

Netsplit A phenomenon which can affect a worldwide real-time chatgroup (as on Internet Relay Chat), where one of the contributing servers loses its connection with the others. The effect is that the group members served by that computer disappear without warning from the chatroom. The reasons for their disappearance emerge only when the connection is restored. >> chatgroup; Internet Relay Chat

network In computing, a group of computers linked together by telecommunications lines for the purpose of working together; for example, the banks are linked by computer networks so that transactions involving more than one bank can be processed between them. For mobile phones, a network is the system of interconnected cells that transmit voice and data between users. It includes all the hardware and software that enables the network to function. >> cell; enterprise computing; Integrated Services Digital Network; Local Area Network; Metropolitan Area Network; network selection; Personal Communications Network; roaming; wireless

network and switching subsystem (NSS) The unit in a GSM (Global System for Mobile Communication) network that controls communications between mobile users and others, both mobile and landline. It also has databases of users and the facilities they subscribe to, and equipment identity numbers. >> Global System for Mobile Communication; International Mobile Equipment Identifier

network selection In mobile communications, a function that enables users to swap between one or more networks when they are travelling across large distances. The selection usually takes place automatically, but can be selected manually. >> network; roaming

newbie A newcomer to a chatgroup or virtual-world environment, especially one who has not yet learned the way to behave when participating in the dialogue. >> chatgroup; netiquette; virtual world

news administrator The designation of the person who manages a Usenet site. >> Usenet

newsgroup >> **chatgroup; USENET**

newt In virtual-world environments, to impose a sanction on a player whose behaviour has been deemed unacceptable, temporarily preventing that player from using his or her screen character; the practice is called **newting**. A more serious sanction is *toading*. >> avatar; toad; virtual world

nick or **nickname** A name adopted by participants in some forms of Internet dialogue, especially in chatgroups and virtual worlds, to preserve their anonymity. Assumed first names (allowing people to use names of either gender), fantasy descriptions (*cooldude*), mythical or fictitious characters (*batman*), and other types are all used. Unlike the use of nicknames in the 'real world', nicks are not permanently owned, but adopted each time one joins a group; nicks may also be changed while one is online, but two members may not use the same nick. >> chatgroup; virtual world

non-linear, nonlinear Term describing a computer or program which is being made to run outside of its normal specifications.
ORIGINAL USE
(as an adjective) *I think I've got a non-linear solution to the problem using Quark.*
NEW USE
(as an adjective, applied to humans) unstable, unpredictable, behaving erratically
That waiter goes non-linear if you query the bill.

no-op An abbreviation for **no operation** – a computer instruction that does nothing.
ORIGINAL USE
(as a noun) *The code has been filled out with several no-ops.*
NEW USE
(as a noun, applied to humans) someone who contributes nothing to a project
Don't waste your time talking to Fred – he's a no-op.
(as a noun, applied to any machine) activity that fails to get the desired result
That stupid no-op has just swallowed my coins and not given me a ticket.

north/south/east/west Compass directions used to navigate around a computer screen when participating in a virtual-world environment. Text commands, such as 'move west', describe the movement of a character in a particular direction. >> virtual world

notebook A term sometimes used for the indexed store of messages which has been sent to a chatgroup. >> chatgroup; log

NSS >> network and switching subsystem

Number Assignment Module (NAM) A function in a mobile phone that stores user information, such as the subscriber identity number. >> mobile phone

numeric A term used to describe devices, such as some pagers, which can only display numbers. >> alphanumeric; pager

O

Office of Telecommunications >> Oftel

offline, off-line Term describing a peripheral device not directly connected to a computer, or temporarily not available; also, a computer not directly connected to a network. >> online

ORIGINAL USE
(as an adjective) *The system allows you to carry out a wide range of offline activities.*

NEW USE
(as an adjective, applied to humans) unavailable, out of touch
She'll be offline for the next few weeks – measles.
He's just totally offline these days. (= he doesn't want to talk to anyone)
(as an adverb) out of public view, somewhere private
Let's go offline for a couple of minutes. (= let's talk privately)

offscreen, off-screen >> onscreen, on-screen

off-topic A term describing the content of a chatgroup conversation which has diverged from the subject-matter that the group was officially set up to address. Several groups use moderators to try to ensure that the members stay focused. However, decisions about what counts as off-topic can be difficult to make, especially in an informal environment, where a certain amount of random subject-matter is to be expected (and often appreciated). >> chatgroup; moderator

Oftel or **Office of Telecommunications** The regulator and supervisory body in charge of the UK telecommunications industry.

-oid A suffix used to express the notion of a 'poor imitation of' or 'approximation to'. Someone trying to be trendy might be described as a *trendoid*; someone who is trying (but failing) to be technologically clever, a *nerdoid*. >> nerd

one-touch dialling >> speed dialling

online, on-line Term describing a peripheral device directly connected to a computer; also, a computer directly connected to a site or network. >> offline
ORIGINAL USE
(as an adjective) *I've found a very useful online resource guide.*
NEW USE
(as an adjective, applied to humans) ready for anything, living life to the full, always around
Sure Jon was at the party; he's one of the most online guys I know.
(also, as an adjective) astute, clued in, on the ball
That's a really cool online remark.

onscreen, on-screen What can be seen on a computer monitor; contrasting with **offscreen** or **off-screen**, for computational activity taking place in background. The term is sometimes used as a synonym of *online*. >> background; online

OOC >> **character**

operating system (OS or **O/S)** A computer program which supervises the running of all other programs on a computer. Common microprocessor operating systems are MS-DOS, Microsoft Windows and Linux.

operator (op) The designation of the person who manages an Internet Relay Chat site. Operators have total control over their channel, deciding who may join it and who may not. >> Internet Relay Chat

OS or **O/S** >> **operating system**

outbox The location in an email facility in which outgoing messages are placed prior to their being sent. >> email

out-of-character >> **character**

P

package assembler disassembler (PAD) >> **packet switching**

packet switching A service provided by Posts, Telegraph and Telephones Authorities which allows one computer to send a message to a second computer in the form of a set of packets transmitted over specially dedicated telephone lines. Packets from different subscribers are all sent down the same line in sequence. This removes the need for the telephone line to be dedicated to the two computers for the whole of the time that they are communicating and is, therefore, much cheaper for the users than a continuous link would be. The mode of operation is akin to sending a letter rather than having a continuous telephone conversation. A **package assembler disassembler** (**PAD**) is a device in data communications which enables a conventional computer to interface to a packet-switching service. >> International Packet Switching Service

PAD >> packet switching

page (**1**) As a noun, a single document on the Web. It includes all the data that can be seen on the screen, once the document has been downloaded, as well as what remains to be seen through scrolling down. >> scrolling; slash; Uniform Resource Locator; Web (**2**) As a verb, a command used in a virtual-world program which enables a character in one room to have a conversation with a character in another room. >> character; room; virtual world

pager Originally, a simple communications device that emitted a beep to alert the user to make contact with a caller, but now a device that can also receive and display short text messages. It is usually small enough to fit into a pocket. >> two-way paging

palmtop >> personal digital assistant

parity check A simple means of detecting errors in transmitted binary data. Each byte contains a **parity bit** which is used to determine whether the number of ones or zeros in the array of bits is odd or even. This bit is then checked on reception to ensure that it is consistent. This simple system will not detect all errors, e.g. it will detect if one bit is in error but not if two are in error. Much more complicated and reliable systems are now in general use. >> ASCII code; binary code; bit; byte

pay as you go In mobile communications, a payment scheme whereby the user purchases a certain amount of airtime in advance (prepaid) either by credit vouchers (available from many types of shops) or by credit/debit-card payment online to the network operator. >> airtime; mobile phone; network

pay monthly In mobile communications, a payment scheme whereby a 12-month contract is agreed between the customer and a network operator, and payments (which include a fixed charge as well as call charges) are made monthly. The fixed charge normally includes some free airtime. >> airtime; mobile phone; network

pay up front In mobile communications, a payment scheme whereby a customer pays for 12 months' line rental in advance. The network in return will offer a quantity of free airtime every month. >> airtime; mobile phone; network

PCMCIA >> **Personal Computer Memory Card International Association**

PCN >> **Personal Communications Network**

PDA >> **personal digital assistant**

persistence The length of time that a conversational message appears on a screen before it scrolls out of sight because of the arrival of other messages. The notion is especially linked to chatgroups, where the persistence is relatively short-lived (compared with traditional writing), though of course messages which have disappeared are often retrievable later by being archived. >> chatgroup; log; scroll

Personal Communications Network (PCN) (1) A short range (less than one mile) communications system using mobile-phone technology. (2) A mobile-phone network complying with the GSM 1800 standard. >> Global System for Mobile Communication; network

Personal Computer Memory Card International Association (PCMCIA) An international trade and standards association that developed the PC card for use with portable computers. >> personal computer

personal computer (PC) A term used to describe microcomputers in general, and also used by the firm of IBM in its range of microcomputers. However, with microcomputers becoming increasingly powerful and widely used in industry and commerce, the initial significance of the term has begun to wane.

personal digital assistant (PDA) A small portable computer that ranges in size from a credit card to a notebook, the most popular being palm-sized; sometimes referred to as a **palmtop** or **handheld computer**. Depending on size, PDAs offer a range of functions from little more than an electronic address book and calculator to almost full personal-computer functionality with Internet access. Smaller units do not have a keyboard, but use buttons or a stylus or even voice to enter data. Most units can be connected to a desktop computer to transfer data. >> functionality; Internet; Pocket PC; wireless

Personal Identification Number (PIN) In mobile communications (as in other electronic access domains), a number that a user has to enter before a call can be made, used as a security measure to prevent unauthorized use; also called a **lock code** or **phone security code**. The expression **PIN number** is widely heard, despite the tautology. >> Personal Unblocking Key

Personal Unblocking Key (PUK) or **PIN unlock code** A security feature for a mobile phone. If a PIN number has been entered incorrectly three times in succession the phone will be locked. The user must obtain the PUK from the service provider to unlock the phone. >> mobile phone; Personal Identification Number

phishing Creating a replica of an existing Web page, usually belonging to a major company, with the intention of fooling someone into passing on sensitive data (such as a password or personal financial details). The term derives from 'fishing', and refers to the way the perpetrators are 'angling' for information. >> hack; spoof (2)

phonebook In mobile communications, a memory module in a phone or on a SIM card where a user can store frequently used numbers with identifiers, so that a number can be selected then dialled automatically. >> SIM card

phone security code >> **Personal Identification Number**

phreaker Someone who uses hacking expertise to gain entry to telephone company computer systems, usually to make free telephone calls; the practice is called **phreaking**. The word is a play on *freak*. >> hacker

PIN >> **Personal Identification Number**

ping (1) Originally, a pulse of sound sent to establish the location of something (especially, the echo sent out by a sonar system); also, to send such a sound pulse. In computing, a message sent from one computer to another to see if it is active and accessible; also, to send such a message.
ORIGINAL USE
(as a noun) *Send a ping to the following site.*
(as a verb) *Use this address if you want to ping our site.*
NEW USE
(as a noun) reminder, contact
Expect a ping from me about 7 o'clock.
(as a verb) get in touch, remind
I'll ping you later. (= I'll get in touch to see if you're in)
(2) In graphics, the informal name of the PNG system. >> digital media

pixel The minimal dot of light from which the images on a computer or television screen are made up; also, the minimal dot of blackness produced by a printer on paper, out of which printed shapes are made up. >> scanner

PLMN >> coverage area

PNG >> digital media

Pocket PC An operating system for personal digital assistants, developed from Windows CE. >> personal digital assistant

poll To check the status of a computer to see if something has been registered.
ORIGINAL USE
(as a verb) *I've just polled my laptop but there's no sign of his message.*

NEW USE
(as a verb) call someone repeatedly
I've been polling Jean all week, but without any response.
(also, as a verb) ask, request
I've polled him for a quick reply.

Portable Network Graphics >> digital media

portal A Web page providing an entry point for sources of information and data from within a site, as well as links to external sites from other providers. >> Web

pose >> emote

post or **posting** A message sent using an email system to a chatgroup or other online forum. The term is also used as a verb: one *posts* a message. >> chatgroup; email

postmaster >> moderator

POTS >> Public Switch Telephone Network

PPS >> Global Positioning System

Precise Positioning Service >> Global Positioning System

predictive text input or **T9** (from 'Text on 9 keys') A function which uses software and a database built into the mobile phone to predict the most likely word being entered as a user presses the keys. Only one key press is required for each letter, and it is the sequence and combination of keys that determines the word displayed. If several words share a combination, the most frequently used word is displayed first and the user can either accept it or use a key to scroll through alternatives. Words can be added to the database. Text entry is much quicker on T9-enabled phones. >> mobile phone; scroll

prepaid >> pay as you go

profiles In mobile communications, functions which are used to personalize the features of a mobile handset. They include level of volume, type of ringtone and message alert tone. >> message alert tone; ringtone

program A sequence of coded instructions in a computer which enables it to carry out a particular operation. Hence, in everyday conversation: **get with the program,** to keep up with an argument, follow the direction of a conversation.

programmer >> wizard

protocol A set of rules built into a computer which specify the way that messages can be sent from the computer to another or to an external device. >> handshake
ORIGINAL USE
(as a noun) *The new protocol has some nice security features built in.*
NEW USE
(as a noun) well-defined procedures of interaction (so that all involved know what they have to do)
Mike's doing protocol with the new members of the team.

PSTN >> Public Switch Telephone Network

Public Land Mobile Network >> coverage area

Public Switch Telephone Network (PSTN) The conventional telephone network provided by the Posts, Telegraph and Telephones Authorities for normal voice communication, often referred to today as **POTS** (Plain Old Telephone Service). Originally an analog service throughout, most networks are now digital except for the link from the consumer to the local exchange, unless the consumer has opted for an ISDN line. >> Integrated Services Digital Network; network

PUK >> **Personal Unblocking Key**

punctuation The traditional set of typographical marks, several of which are used in additional ways in email messaging. At one extreme, there are emails which avoid punctuation other than spacing. Most emails are lightly punctuated, relying on the full-stop or spacing as the main grammatical marker, and making a limited use of commas, and hardly any use of semi-colons and colons. By contrast, question-marks and exclamation-marks can be used repeatedly, as expressions of emphasis, e.g. *hey!!!!!!!*. Pairs of asterisks or underbars are sometimes used for emphasis (e.g. *the *real* issue*), as is letter spacing (e.g. *the question is w h y*). Angle brackets and slash-marks are also used with a variety of functions. The iconic properties of punctuation marks are exploited in emoticons. >> angle brackets; asterisk; emoticon; hash; slash; underbar

R

radiofrequency (RF) A term describing the sector of the electromagnetic spectrum between the audible range and visible light, about 30 kHz to 300 mHz. >> hertz; specific absorption rate

RAM or **random access memory, read-and-write memory** A type of computer memory, usually integrated circuits, which can be read from and written to. RAM is used in all computers; data contained in RAM is lost when the electrical power is removed. >> memory

random access memory >> **RAM**

read-and-write memory >> **RAM**

readme, README, occasionally **read me, read-me** A file of explanatory information accompanying a software program, which new users are advised to read as a preliminary.

ORIGINAL USE

(as an adjective) *You should definitely take a look at the readme file before trying to send anything.*

(as a noun) *The changes are listed in the new version of README.*

NEW USE

(as a noun) manual, set of instructions

Anybody seen the readme for the lawn-mower?

read-only memory >> **ROM**

reboot To shut down a computer and start it up again.

ORIGINAL USE

(as a verb) *After you've loaded the new software, you have to reboot.*

(as a noun) *I've just done a reboot and the program still doesn't work.*

NEW USE

(as a verb, applied to humans) start again from scratch

Hey, reboot a minute – you're going too fast for me.

remailer >> anonymizer

reverse billing An emerging service offered by mobile-phone service providers whereby users can pay for products and services by adding the charge to their phone account or having the amount deducted from their prepaid credit. It is particularly aimed at a market sector where low-value or micro-payment transactions (pence or cents rather than pounds or dollars) are the norm. >> airtime; mobile phone; network

RF >> radiofrequency

roaming The ability to operate a mobile phone on a different network from the one the user has suscribed to. If a mobile phone cannot connect to the network owned by the user's mobile service provider, it will attempt to connect to any other compatible network within range. The connection will only be accepted if the two networks have a **roaming agreement**. The phone companies will then exchange information about the usage, and the home operator will charge the user for the calls made and received on the other network. Roaming is more expensive than calls made through the home operator, and the user has to pay an extra charge for incoming calls. >> network selection

ROM or **read-only memory, readonly memory** A type of computer memory, usually integrated circuits, which can only be read from; the data is fixed during the manufacture of the chip. ROM is used where the data does not have to be altered; the data also remains intact even if the electrical power is removed. >> firmware; memory
RELATED USE
(as an adjective) *The data from that newsgroup is now read-only.*

NEW USE

(as an adjective, applied to humans) unmoveable, unwilling to listen

No point in talking to Art – he's readonly when it comes to salary levels.

room (1) An Internet site which members of a chatgroup join when they are online. (2) A functional space within a virtual world, described according to the theme of that world. A room might be a castle, a city, a space station, a road, or any imaginary analogue of a real-world location. The properties of rooms are textually described within the database. >> chatgroup; virtual world

S

sanity check The act of checking a piece of code for really stupid errors, such as missing out a slash-mark or a bracket; also widely used as a management procedure in test situations outside of computing (e.g. *Each chapter of the book concludes with a sanity check*).

ORIGINAL USE

(as a noun) *The program loads a simple piece of software which does a sanity check before letting you do anything.*

NEW USE

(as a noun, in relation to a conversation) request for confirmation that the participants are talking about the same thing, or making the same assumptions

Hold on a minute, sanity check, are we talking about the same car?

SAR >> specific absorption rate

scanner An input device in a computer system which scans documents and transfers a map of the document into the memory of the computer. The document is represented by an array of pixels, with the number of pixels per square inch of document signifying the quality of the scanner. Low-quality scanners scan only black and white at 300 pixels per square inch (i.e. 90,000 per square inch); high-quality ones scan in full colour at 1200 pixels per inch. In each element of the array a value is stored to represent the colour and brightness of that pixel. Most scanners are accompanied by software which can analyse the page image, pick out blocks of text, and convert the image into a text string. >> pixel

screen saver A program that causes the image on a computer, personal digital assistant, or mobile-phone screen to change if there has been no keyboard or mouse input for a predetermined length of time. Originally designed to prevent a fixed image becoming etched or burned onto the screen, they are more of an entertainment or artistic utility now, as modern screens are much more robust.

scribble A feature used in some chatroom environments which allows senders to delete a message after it has been sent, perhaps because they realize it is off-topic or contains unintentionally offensive language. >> chatgroup

scrolling The vertical displacement of information which occurs when reading a page that is larger than what can be seen on a single computer screen. New material appears at the bottom of the screen at the same rate as material at the top of the screen disappears. >> page

search engine A resource on the Web, accessible via a browser, which helps a user to find sites and information. Search engines continually traverse the Web (using programs known as **spiders**), following links that are built into documents, and building up indexes of material – for example, recovering titles, headings, and subheadings, important words, and lines from documents. Manipulation of the indexes is carried out using standard techniques of information retrieval, and the continual traversal ensures that the indexes are routinely updated. The indexes enable search engines to locate many of the documents related to a particular search topic. However, most searches retrieve large numbers of irrelevant documents, within which relevant 'hits' can be lost, and a great deal of effort is currently being devoted to finding ways of improving search results. >> browser; Web

second-generation >> generation

second-level domain (SLD) The set of Internet names recognized within a top-level domain, relating to different types of activity, such as the *co* in *bbc.co.uk*. The *co* abbreviation identifies UK commercial enterprises; *ac* is used for UK educational enterprises; there is a complete list on p. 177. >> domain name system; top-level domain

Secure Electronic Transaction (SET) A standard for secure payment transactions over the Internet or other electronic networks. >> Internet

security code >> Personal Identification Number

sent folder A location in an email facility which lists the emails that have been sent out from that particular address. >> email

server A network computer that provides a service to client computer users. A wide range of functions is involved, such as the sending and receiving of emails, providing access to the Web or chatroom sites, offering space for constructing Web pages, and making available files of data. >> chatgroup; client/server; email; network; Web

service provider In the Internet and telecommunications, the company that provides access to a network and charges a user for the service. In many cases the network operator and the service provider are the same company. >> Internet Service Provider; network

SET >> **Secure Electronic Transaction**

SGML >> **Hypertext Markup Language**

Short Messaging Service (SMS), texting, or **text-messaging** A GSM (Global System for Mobile Communication) service that enables a user to send short text messages to other mobile users. The service uses the control channels, which allows a message to arrive while a voice call is in progress, but limits the length of the message to a maximum of 160 characters. >> Global System for Mobile Communication; smart messaging; p. 139

SIM card An abbreviation for **Subscriber Identity Module card**: a smart card that fits into a GSM (Global System for Mobile Communication) phone and gives the user access to the mobile network. The SIM card contains a number of security functions, and it is possible to use it to save information such as names and telephone numbers. Future developments will add more facilities to the SIM card, allowing greater personalization of the phone and its use. >> Global System for Mobile Communication; mobile phone; SIM lock

SIM lock An abbreviation for **Subscriber Identity Module lock**: software that locks a phone to a specific SIM card and network. The phone will not work if a different SIM card is inserted. >> mobile phone; SIM card

sketchphone A system, linked to the telephone network, by which line drawings and sketches can be transmitted long distances to suitable receiving equipment. An electronic touch-sensitive screen sends sketches via a computer and the telephone line to a receiver.

slash or **forward slash** In Web addresses, the character which separates the various levels of pages of information available at a site. >> domain name; dot; Web

SLD >> second-level domain

smart messaging or **enhanced messaging service (EMS)** In mobile communications, a system which delivers Short Messaging Service messages with a limited number of added features, such as business cards, or ringtone and profile downloads. >> profiles; Short Messaging Service

Smartphone A 3G device that is a combination of a mobile phone and a personal digital assistant. >> generation; personal digital assistant

smiley >> emoticon

SMS >> Short Messaging Service

smurf / smurfette A member of a chatgroup (male and female, respectively) who regularly sends messages to the group which have little or no interesting content. >> chatgroup

sorg An abbreviation of **straight or gay**, often used in chatrooms as a query message when the receiver wants to know the sexual orientation of the sender. There is of course no way of knowing whether the subsequent clarification is truthful. >> morf

south >> **north/south/east/west**

spam (1) An off-topic and usually lengthy message sent to a chatgroup; also, to send such a message. (2) Junk email sent to many recipients; also, to send such mail. **Spamming** is the practice of sending unwanted messages in these ways; the people who carry out this practice are called **spammers**. The term originates in a 1970 Monty Python sketch about a cafe in which the availability of dishes was totally dependent on the presence of quantities of the tinned meat, spam. >> chatgroup; email

ORIGINAL USE

(as a noun) *I got twenty emails this morning, and eighteen of them were spam.*

(as a verb) *That firm spams me virtually every day with the same piece of rubbish.*

NEW USE

(as a noun) lengthy and unwanted utterance, especially in an attempt to advertise or sell something

I can't stand the spam they put into those commercial breaks.

(as a verb) speak intrusively and at length, especially in an attempt to advertise or sell something

I phoned a helpline, but the guy just spammed me about their latest products.

(also, as a noun) irrelevant, intrusive, or evasive remark

I asked for my money but he just gave me a pile of spam and told me to come back next week.

(also, as a verb) make an irrelevant, intrusive, or evasive remark
Stop spamming me, will you? I can make my own mind up.

spammer Someone who sends off-topic messages to a newsgroup; later: an individual or organization that sends junk email to many recipients.
ORIGINAL USE
(as a noun) *How do spammers find out all those email addresses?*
NEW USE
(as a noun) someone who speaks intrusively and at length, especially in an attempt to advertise or sell something
I only wanted a brochure, but got caught by a spammer and it took me ten minutes to get away.
(also, as a noun) someone who continually makes irrelevant, intrusive, or evasive remarks
I'm starting to avoid John; he's turning into a real spammer these days.

specific absorption rate (SAR) The amount of energy absorbed by a human body from a radiofrequency source. Many national regulatory bodies are now requiring mobile-phone manufacturers to carry out SAR tests on their products to ensure they comply with that nation's guidelines. An international standard has not yet been defined, and some scientific bodies have disputed the value of the tests and the results achieved. >> radiofrequency

speed dialling or **one-touch dialling** A function available on many fixed and mobile-phone handsets that enables the user to store telephone numbers in numbered memory locations, then later to dial a selected telephone number using the much shorter location number.

spider >> search engine

spoof (**1**) In Internet chat situations, a message whose origin or content is suspect; also, to send such a message; the practice is called **spoofing**. In a fantasy-game environment, for example, a message might say that a certain player has been eaten by a lion, whereas no such thing has happened. Spoofers usually introduce their remarks for fun, thereby introducing an element of anarchy into the conversation. Spoofing is common in the game environments of virtual worlds, though not all groups approve of the practice. >> chatgroup; troll; virtual world (**2**) The term is also used for a hacking technique which tries to bypass security measures on a network by imitating a computer address or the operation of an element of the network's hardware or software. >> hack; phising

SPS >> Global Positioning System

stack A set of locations in a computer which store data in such a way that the most recently stored item is the first to be retrieved; also, a list of the items stored in this way (a *push-down* list).
ORIGINAL USE
The device monitors stack levels to avoid overflow.
NEW USE
(as a noun, applied to humans) set of things someone has to do
Washing the car is way down my stack.
You've finally got to the top of my stack.
(also, as a noun) memory capacity, ability to handle information
Sorry, my stack just overflowed. (= Too many points have just been made, and I've lost track of the ones made some time ago)

Standard Generalized Markup Language >> Hypertext Markup Language

Standard Positioning Service >> Global Positioning System

standby time The length of time (usually stated in hours) in which a powered-on phone stays charged and is therefore theoretically capable of making and receiving calls. A phone on standby is not completely idle; it is listening on the control channels, which requires much less power than that needed to make a call. A phone with a long standby time may nevertheless have a short calling time, as the increased power demand rapidly discharges the battery. >> mobile phone

state The situation achieved at a certain point in a computational process, which determines what output it produces for a given input.
ORIGINAL USE
In this state you can use two applications at once, but not three.
NEW USE
(as a noun, applied to humans) condition, situation
What's your state? (= what are you doing? what's happening next? how are you doing?)

stop word A word which is so frequent and contains so little semantic information (usually because it performs a grammatical role in a sentence) that a search mechanism is programmed to ignore it. Typical stop words include *a*, *and*, *the* and *of*. Problems arise when such words have homonyms which do contain semantic content, such as *OR* (the abbreviation for *Oregon*). >> search engine

streaming A term used to describe the continuous transmission of data from one device to another. **Streaming audio** involves the sending of an uninterrupted sound sequence over a data network and **streaming video** the sending of an uninterrupted video sequence. Both notions are encompassed by the phrase **streaming media**, which anticipates the ongoing simultaneous transmission of any combination of media from a source device to a receiver. In such contexts, users can access the data while it is being sent, and lose it once the receiving device is shut down. By contrast, in a system which allows you to access a sound or video sequence (such as a movie) only after it has been completely downloaded, the download remains in your computer when the device is closed. >> bandwidth; multimedia

Subscriber Identity Module >> **SIM card; SIM lock**

surf To explore sites on the Internet in general, or on the Web in particular.

Symbian >> **EPOC**

synchronous (**1**) A term describing chatgroups where the discussions take place in real time, as with Internet Relay Chat. (**2**) More generally, in telecommunications, describing data which is transmitted in real time, such as a fax or a telephone conversation. >> chatgroup; Internet Relay Chat

T9 >> **predictive text input**

TACS >> **Total Access Communications System**

tags The codes enclosed in angle brackets used in markup languages (such as HTML, SGML, XML) to identify sections of text. In HTML the codes are predefined and relate specifically to how the text is displayed, whereas in SGML and XML the user can define the codes within the document, or more usually in an accompanying document called a Document Type Description (DTD). >> Extensible Markup Language; Hypertext Markup Language

talktime >> **airtime**

teleport A command used in a virtual-world program which enables a character to move at will from one room to another. >> character; room; virtual world

texting >> **Short Messaging Service**

text messaging >> **messaging; Short Messaging Service**

third-generation >> **generation**

thread A sequence of messages arranged on the basis of their contribution to a single topic. Threads can be seen when email messages are arranged according to their subject-lines, and are also noticeable in the way contributions to online discussion groups are often presented. >> chatroom; log

three-G, third generation, usually written **3G** >> **generation**

three-way calling, usually written **3-way calling** In mobile-phone communications, a system that allows three parties to share a conversation. >> mobile phone

thumbnail In Web graphics, a screen version of a larger image which is much smaller and of lower resolution than its large counterpart. It also loads much more quickly. In many cases, the viewer can click on the image to see the large version. >> Web

tinker >> wizard

TinyMUD >> MUD

TLD >> top-level domain

toad In virtual-world environments, to impose a sanction on a player whose behaviour has been deemed unacceptable, altering that player's screen character so that it appears ugly, preventing it from carrying out certain functions, or even completely excluding it from the game; the practice is called **toading**. It is a more serious sanction than newting. >> newt; virtual world

top-level domain (TLD) The name which occurs at the top of the Internet domain-name hierarchy – the rightmost element of a domain name. Examples include **country codes** such as *uk* in *bbc.co.uk* or non-geographical **generic codes** such as *org* in *www.icann.org*. Within countries, regional administrators control what second-level domains are recognized. Most US addresses, for historical reasons, do not end in a country code. See the list on p. 179. >> domain name system; second-level domain

Total Access Communications System (TACS) The analog system used in the UK and a number of other countries, operating in the 900 Mhz band. It is similar to AMPS, used in the USA. >> Advanced Mobile Phone System

tri-band A term describing a mobile phone that is capable of operating on three frequency bands: 900 Mhz, 1800 Mhz and 1900 Mhz. >> band; Global System for Mobile Communication; hertz

troll In Internet chat situations, a message specifically intended to cause irritation to other members of the group; the practice is called **trolling**. Trolls are usually innocent-sounding questions or statements, delivered deadpan, and usually containing false information; the originator then sits back and waits to see the explosive reactions of the group. The term derives from fishing (the trailing of a hook to see what bites), though it also captures the resonance of the trolls of Scandinavian mythology – the bridge-guarders who would let people pass only if they answered a question correctly. If someone does fall for the troll, they may receive the message *YHBT* (= You Have Been Trolled). Not all groups approve of the practice. >> chatgroup

two-G, second generation, usually written **2G** >> **generation**

two-way messaging >> **two-way paging**

two-way paging or **two-way messaging** A development in paging technology, particularly in the USA, that allows users to both receive and send text messages of up to 500 characters. The advantage over 2G mobile phones is the smaller size of the pager, much longer battery life, and in the USA the possibilty of national coverage from a single service provider. The technology can also be applied to personal digital assistants. >> generation; pager; personal digital assistant

typist >> **character**

U

UMTS >> Universal Mobile Telecommunications System

underbar (_) A keyboard symbol which has developed a range of functions in Internet communication. It is often used as a way of formally linking elements in an address, without adding any meaning, such as *David_ Crystal*. Pairs of underbars are also sometimes used around words in emails to express emphasis, e.g. *the _real_ point*.

Uniform Resource Locator (URL) The distinct address that identifies each resource on the Internet. Different 'pages' of data at a site are distinguished by means of labels separated by forward slashes. URLs can be of considerable length, as a consequence. >> Internet; page; slash; Web

Universal Mobile Telecommunications System (UMTS) In mobile communications, a 3G standard being developed by the European Telecommunications Standards Institute as a major part of the International Telecommunication Union's IMT-2000 specification. Operating in the 2 Ghz band, it promises to offer data transmission speeds of 2 Mbs, and to interface seamlessly with satellite communications systems to give global coverage. >> European Telecommunications Standards Institute; generation; IMT-2000

Universal Terrestrial Radio Access (UTRA) The European Telecommunications Standards Institute proposal for the radio technology needed to deliver the Universal Mobile Telecommunications System. >> Universal Mobile Telecommunications System

unlock code >> Personal Unlocking Key

upload >> download

Usenet (1) Originally, a term referring to a network of computers all running the Unix operating system and each communicating with the others. (2) A worldwide system of Internet groups (known as *newsgroups*) enabling participants to discuss a very wide range of topics. Over fifty major domains deal with such areas as recreation, science, business, computing and news, each of which contains varying numbers of subgroups, organized in a hierarchy. Discussions are carried on asynchronously. >> asynchronous; chatgroup; Internet

usergroup >> chatgroup

UTRA >> Universal Terrestrial Radio Access

V- An abbreviation for **virtual**, as encountered in such words as *V-chat* (= virtual chat).

virtual world On the Internet, an imaginary environment which people can enter to engage in text-based social interaction. The environments can be constructed for a variety of purposes, such as the ludic (fantasy games and adventure worlds) and the educational (e.g. role-playing business management interactions), or simply to make social contact. Depending on the perception of the kind of activity involved, participants in virtual worlds are called *users* or *players*. A distinction is drawn between the users/players and the *characters* they create onscreen. >> character; MOO; MUD

voice dial A hands-free facility for dialling a number. The user stores a telephone number with a **voice tag** (a short spoken message) that is then used to identify the number to be dialled when the tag is spoken.

voicemail An answering service operated by a service provider where a caller can leave a message if unable to connect to the phone being called. Various methods are used to indicate to a subscriber that messages have been stored, such as an icon appearing on the handset screen, a short text message, or a call from the answering system. >> asynchronous 2

voice memo A voice recorder built in to a phone that can be used independently or during a phone conversation. Recording conversations in this way is illegal in some countries.

voice tag >> voice dial

W

WAP >> Wireless Application Protocol

WAP Forum An industry association founded by Nokia, Ericsson, Motorola and Phone.com to develop standards for delivering multimedia content to mobile phones. They are responsible for the Wireless Application Protocol. A large number of IT and telephone companies have joined the WAP Forum, and almost every company working with the mobile Internet is represented. >> Wireless Application Protocol

WAP gateway The link between the mobile and traditional Internet. It is a server that converts sets of data in Wireless

Markup Language into a compact binary format for transmission over the mobile net to the cellular phone, and vice versa. >> gateway; server; Wireless Application Protocol; Wireless Markup Language

WAP Internet Service Provider (WISP) A company that provides access to WAP content on the Internet. >> Internet; Wireless Application Protocol

WAP sites Pages of data (analogous to those on a Web site) viewable on a WAP-enabled device. >> page; Web; Wireless Application Protocol

warez Illegally copied or pirated software. This is usually computer application software, but may be any pirated digital media. Typically, a Web-site devoted to warez downloads might contain software, music files and copyrighted images. There is a tendency among the distributors of warez to append a -z to any word to denote its illegal provenance. Thus there are Web-sites containing *tunez*, *gamez*, *serialz*, *filez*, *crackz* and others. Warez, however, is the umbrella term.

WAV >> digital media

Web or **World Wide Web, WWW,** or **W3** The full collection of all the computers linked to the Internet which hold documents that are mutually accessible through use of a standard protocol (the HyperText Transfer Protocol, HTTP); in site addresses presented as the acronym **www.** The creator of the Web, British computer scientist Tim Berners-Lee (1955–), has defined it as the 'universe of network-accessible information, an embodiment of human knowledge'. It was devised in 1990 as a means of enabling high-energy physicists in different institutions to share information within their field, but it rapidly spread to other fields, and is now all-inclusive. A **Web site** is an individual computer holding documents capable of being transferred to and presented by browsers, using one of the standard formats (usually HTML or XML). Web sites are identified by a unique address, or **URL** (**Uniform Resource Locator**). Anything that can exist as a computer file can be made available as a Web document – text, graphics, sound, video, etc. A further necessary element of the Web is the search engine, a means of locating documents by content rather than by location. >> document description language; Internet; search engine; Uniform Resource Locator; Web-; Web clipping; World Wide Web Consortium

Web- A prefix designating an entity, event, or other phenomenon which relates to the World Wide Web. Hundreds of coinages have been made since the early 1990s, such as *webcast*, *webmail*, *webliography*, *webmaster*, *webonomics*, *webzine* and *webhead* (= web addict). >> Web

Web clipping The process of minimizing the amount of data from a Web site transferred to a mobile phone in response to a query, developed by Palm for their personal digital assistants. >> personal digital assistant; Web

Weblish >> Netlish

welcome note A personalized text or image reference that appears when a mobile handset is powered up. >> mobile phone

WELL or **Whole Earth 'Lectronic Link** A worldwide system of Internet groups (known as *conferences*), founded in 1985, enabling participants to discuss a very wide range of topics. Discussions are carried on asynchronously. >> asynchronous; chatgroup; Internet

west >> **north/south/east/west**

whisper A command used in a virtual-world program which enables a character to have a conversation with another character in the same room, without other characters being aware of what is said. >> character; room; virtual world

whois (= Who Is?) A type of command used in interrogating certain Web and chatgroup sites, which provides information about the participating members. >> chatgroup; Web

Whole Earth 'Lectronic Link >> **WELL**

Wide Area Network >> **Local Area Network**

Wi-Fi or **WiFi** [wai-fai] An abbreviation of **wireless fidelity,** a standard ensuring the interworking of equipment in a wireless network. >> wireless

wildcard, wild card A character that will match any other character or combination of characters which occur at a particular point in a string, usually symbolized by an asterisk or question-mark. A search for *d*t*, for example, would elicit *dat, det, d3t, duct, doublet*, etc.

win >> **lose**

Windows Waveform >> **digital media**

wired Using wires (or a similar connection) to carry an electrical signal; then, in computing, linked to a computer network. >> hardwired

ORIGINAL USE

(as an adjective) *As cables enter millions of homes, we are becoming a wired nation.*

[advertisement] *Get wired and find out all the latest jobs.*

NEW USE

(as an adjective, applied to humans) ready, alert, capable of handling a point

I explained what I was doing, but I don't think Max was wired enough to take it all in.

RELATED USE

wired up, ready, alert, capable of handling a point
Are you wired up for the latest episode in Jane's saga?

wireless A term describing the products and standards which allow electronic communication to take place without electrical connections (wires or cables). A wide range of applications uses wireless technology, including home products (e.g. TV remotes, garage-door control), radio-frequency identification devices (for tracking people, animals, or objects), voice and text communicators (e.g. mobile phones, cordless phones, pagers), and global positioning systems. Its use is especially growing in relation to remote data acquisition (e.g. for personal digital assistants) and computer networking (e.g. in Local Area Networks). A location which offers a wireless connection to the Internet is known as a 'hotspot'. >> Global Positioning System; Local Area Network; mobile phone

Wireless Application Protocol (WAP) A system for advanced data-transfer on the mobile Internet. WAP contains standards for data-compression, data-transfer, security, page design and more, and has been developed to work on devices with small screens and limited processing power. The development of WAP is controlled by the WAP Forum. >> Internet; WAP Forum; WAP gateway; wireless; Wireless Markup Language

Wireless Markup Language (WML) A markup language, based on XML, designed for use on mobile phones and pagers with their small display screens, limited memory and processing ability, and limited user input facilities. The data is arranged in **cards**, where one card contains data to fill a typical screen; and cards are grouped as **decks**, which are transmitted to the mobile phone. WML controls navigation between the cards and decks. >> Extensible Markup Language; wireless; WMLScript

WISP >> **WAP Internet Service Provider**

wizard A common designation for the system administrator who manages a virtual world environment (a MUD or MOO). A wide range of alternatives exist, such as **programmers, tinkers, gods, arches,** and **imps** (= implementers). To become a wizard requires in-depth experience of a site, and usually also some programming ability. Wizards have considerable disciplinary powers over the other participants and a great deal of discretion to make technical decisions. >> virtual world

WMLScript A programming language for use in Wireless Markup Language cards. It is very similar to JavaScript used in HTML pages, but is much simpler. >> Hypertext Markup Language; Wireless Markup Language

World Wide Web Consortium (W3C) A non-profit organization that oversees the evolution of the Web by developing and issuing specifications and guidelines to ensure inter-operability. It is responsible for HTML and XML, among other specifications. >> Extensible Markup Language; Hypertext Markup Language; Web

W3 >> **Web**

W3C >> **World Wide Web Consortium**

WWW >> **Web**

X

XHTML >> **Hypertext Markup Language**

XML >> **Extensible Markup Language**

Y

YOYOW (= **You Own Your Own Words**) An aphorism used by the WELL chatgroup stressing the element of personal responsibility in maintaining an atmosphere of mutual respect and co-operation in chatroom discussions. >> chatgroup; WELL

Z

-z A noun plural inflection which replaces the standard -*s* when the noun refers to a pirated version of software. >> warez

An A-to-Z of Emoticons (Smileys)

Receiving: Symbols to Meanings

The notion of 'A to Z' is irrelevant when dealing with non-alphabetic symbols. To find an item in the following list, we need to decide upon a sorting order. In this book, sorting is based on symbol sequence, starting at the left, in the order shown below.

For example, the emoticon :-(*) can be read as 'colon, hyphen, opening round bracket, asterisk, closing round bracket'. It will therefore be found in the 'Colon set', at the point where the second element is a hyphen (the fourteenth item down in the list below).

Emoticons have an intriguing existence. Very few of them are ever used. Surveys of email and chatgroups suggest that only about 10 per cent of messages actually use them, and then usually just the two basic types – :) and :(. Yet they still exercise a fascination: as an art form, or for entertainment, large numbers have been invented, and continue to be. Whole stories, using long sequences of emoticons, have been devised. The following list is not exhaustive, therefore, but it is certainly representative of what is 'out there'.

colon	:
semi-colon	;
period	.
comma	,
question-mark	?

exclamation-mark	!
apostrophe	'
hyphen	-
opening round bracket	(
closing round bracket	)
opening square bracket	[
closing square bracket	]
opening curly bracket	{
closing curly bracket	}
opening angle bracket	<
closing angle bracket	>
tilde	~
asterisk	*
backslash	\
forward slash	/
pipe	|
underbar	_
caret	^
percentage	%
ampersand	&
at	@
hash	#
equals	=
plus	+
zero	0
numerals	1, 2 etc.
letters	A, B etc.

Colon set

:'-)	happy and crying
:'-(	sad and crying
:' (	sad and crying
:')	happy and crying
:-	male
:-...	heart-broken

:-,	smirking
:-?	smoking a pipe
:-!	bland
:----)	Pinocchio
:-(	unhappy, sad, dissatisfied, frowning
:-( )	mouth open, shocked, awed, amazed
:-(>~	goatee
:-(*)	feeling sick
:-(O)	yelling
:-)	happy, joking, smiling, satisfied
:-):-):-)	guffawing loudly
:-))	very happy
:-))))))))	ecstatic
:-)~	drooling
:-)~~~~~<	beam me up
:-)=	bearded
:-)8	wearing bow tie
:-[	critical, disgusted, determined, pouting
:-[	vampire
:-]	obnoxious, sarcastic
:-]	jaw hitting the ground with shock
:-{)	moustache
:-{}	blowing a kiss
:-{}	lipstick
:-}	leering, wry, tipsy
:-<	cheated, forlorn, sad
:-<>	surprised
:->	devilish, sarcastic
:-~)	got a cold
:-*	bitter, sour
:-*	kiss
:-\	sceptical, undecided
:-/	perplexed, puzzled, confused
:-|	indifferent, apathetic
:-|	puzzled, perplexed

:-‖	angry
:-&	tongue-tied
:-@	cursing, swearing
:-@	screaming
:-# :-X	lips sealed
:-#		bushy moustache
:-0	uh-oh; silent
:-1	bland, smirking
:-6	sour, exhausted
:-7	wry
:-8(	condescending
:-9	delicious, yummy
:-C	unbelieving, couldn't care less
:-c	very unhappy
:-D	laughing
:-E	buck-toothed vampire
:-h	forked tongue
:-J	tongue in cheek
:-O	mouth open, very surprised, amazed
:-o	shocked, amazed, appalled
:-ozz	bored
:-P	tongue out, panting in anticipation
:-Q	smoking
:-T	straight-faced
:-v	talking
:-W	forked tongue
:-w	forked tongue
:-X	sworn to secrecy, lips sealed
:-X	big kiss, snogging you
:-x	sworn to secrecy
:-x	kiss
:(	unhappy, sad, dissatisfied, frowning
:( )	can't stop talking
:)	happy, joking, smiling, satisfied
:~-(	crying a lot

:~(~~	crying lots and lots
:~~)	got a bad cold
:~/	mixed up
:*}	tipsy, drunk
:/)	not amused
:_(	punched on the nose
:^)	tongue in cheek, clowning
:^)	broken nose
:^o	broken nose hurting
:@	shouting
:=(	two noses and sad
:=)	two noses and happy
:=8)	baboon
:O	amazed, surprised, shocked
:o(	sad, unhappy, dissatisfied
:o)	happy, joyful
:o)}	goatee
:o{)	moustache
:ol	couldn't care less
:o#	wearing braces
:P	disgusted (sticking out tongue)

Semi-colon set

;-)	winking
;-}	leering
;->	devilish wink, lewd
;-P	tongue in cheek
;)	winking
;>)	smirking
;^)	smirking
;o)	joking

Period set

.-(	lost a contact lens
.._(:)-)	scuba diver

.._( )-)	scuba diver with a broken mask
.o+|(=:	ballerina

Question-mark set

?:o)	wavy hair parted on one side

Exclamation-mark set

!:-)	imaginative

Apostrophe set

'-)	winking

Hyphen set

-:-)	punk
-(D)	astronaut
-]:-)[-	impressed
-\V/	go forth and prosper [Vulcan salute]
-0.06	not very clever

Opening round bracket set

(::()::)	bandaid
(:-(	very unhappy
(:-)	wearing helmet
(:-\ :-<	sad
(:+(	scared
(;.;)/~	waving goodbye
(-)	haircut, needs
(-_-)	me
(-o-)	imperial TIE fighter
(( )):**	hugs and kisses
(((-_-)))	Cartman
(((><)))	Kenny
(((o-o)))	got my hood up
(((((name))))	hug [cyber hug]
(>:[X	Count Dracula

(>_<)	angry
(*-*)	Pokemon
(*_*)	falling in love
(_._)	moonie
(_)	mug (of coffee, beer)
(^.^)/	waving hello
(^O^)	singing
(@_@)	boggle-eyed
(=_=)	sleepy
(OvO)	owl
(o^-^o)	Pikachu

Closing round bracket set
):-)	impish

Opening square bracket set
[:-)	wearing walkman
[:=l]	Frankenstein
[8-*	Maggie Simpson

Closing square bracket set
]B-)	Batman

Opening curly bracket set
{:-)	hair parted down the middle
{:-)	toupee
{:-{	very unhappy
{:<>	Daffy Duck
{8-)	Lisa Simpson

Closing curly bracket set
}:-(	toupee blowing in the wind
}:-)	devilish
}:-}	big grin
};->	rude devil

Opening angle bracket set

<:-l	monk
<:oO	dunce
<l-)	Chinese

Closing angle bracket set

>:-(	angry
>:-)	devilish
>:->	leering
>:o)	Devil
>;-)	evil thought
>;->	rude suggestions
>-	female
>-::-D	smitten by Cupid's arrow
>-)	rude devil
>(::o>	alien
>>>:-]	Klingon
>8o!	Bugs Bunny with a carrot

Tilde set

~(_8^(l)	Homer Simpson
~~o	let's make babies
~//(^o^)/~/~	octopus
~8-)	Harry Potter

Asterisk set

* :-o	alarmed
*-)	stoned
*<:-)	Santa Claus, Father Christmas
* * * *	popcorn
*8((:	strange

Backslash set

\-o	bored
\~/	full glass

_/	glass (of drink)
'\=o-o=/'	wearing glasses

Forward slash set

/:-I	Mr Spock

Pipe set

I:-I	absolutely rigid
I-(3-i	asleep and having nightmares
I-)	sniggering
I-/	constipated
I-I	asleep
I-O	snoring, yawning
I-P	very revolted
I-p	revolted
IIII8^)X	Cat in the Hat
I^o	snoring
ICI	can of Coke
Io	me asleep
IoO	lost a contact lens
IPI	can of Pepsi

Underbar set

__,,,^..^,,,__	Harry Potter
___2_2222___	Flintstone, Fred

Caret set

^	thumbs up
^5	high five

Percentage set

%')	drunk
%-(	confused and unhappy
%-)	confused but happy
%-{	sad

%-{ :/)	not amused
%-}	drunk
%-<l>	confused but happy
%-\	hungover
%-/	hungover
%-6	not very clever
%*}	drunk
%*@:-)	hungover
%+(	unconscious

Ampersand set

&:-)	curly hair
&.(..	crying a lot
&&&&	pretzels

At set

@:-)	wearing turban
@;-)	flirt
@--)--)(--	rose
@->-	rose
@(*0*)@	koala bear
@[_]~~	mug of very hot coffee or tea
@}--\-,---	rose
@@@@8-)	Marge Simpson

Hash set

#:-)	wearing fur hat
#:oO	tangled hair
#-l #-(	

Equals set

=:-)	punk
=:-o	hair-raising experience
=-0~~~~	Starship *Enterprise* firing phasers
=-0***	Starship *Enterprise* firing photon torpedoes

=(8-0)	hair-raising experience
=) 8-(	surprised
=l:-)=	Uncle Sam

Plus sign set

+-(:-)>+	Pope
+<#^v	night
+0:-)	Pope

Zero set

0	Starship *Enterprise*
0:-)	angel
0:o)	angel

Numerals set

3:-)	Bart Simpson
3:*>	Rudolph the Rednosed Reindeer
3-I	asleep and having nightmares
3-O	snoring
7:n)	Fred Flintstone
8:-)	glasses on forehead
8-)	wearing glasses
8-)	wide-eyed smile
8-]	in love
8->	just happy
8-l	in suspense
8-#	dead
8(:-)	Mickey Mouse
8^(	sad
8^l	grim
8o)	wearing glasses

Letters set

B:-)	wearing sunglasses
B-)	wearing sunglasses

C¦:-)	wearing bowler hat
d:-)	wearing cap
P-)	fresh
X-(	dead
X-)	unconscious
X-#	dead

Sending: Meanings of Symbols

absolutely rigid	¦:-¦
alarmed	* :-o
alien	>(::o>
amazed, surprised, shocked	:O
angel	0:-)
angel	0:o)
angry	:-¦ ¦
angry	(>_<)
angry	>:-(
asleep	¦-I
asleep and having nightmares	¦-(3-i
asleep and having nightmares	3-I
astronaut	-(D)
baboon	:=8)
ballerina	.o+¦(=:
bandaid	(::()::)
Bart Simpson	3:-)
Batman	]B-)
beam me up	:-)~~~~~<
bearded	:-)=
big grin	}:-}
big kiss, snogging you	:-X
bitter, sour	:-*
bland	:-!
bland, smirking	:-1
blowing a kiss	:-{}

boggle-eyed	(@_@)
bored	:-ozz
bored	\-o
broken nose	:^)
broken nose hurting	:^o
buck-toothed vampire	:-E
Bugs Bunny with a carrot	>8o!
bushy moustache	:-#	
can of Coke	|C|
can of Pepsi	|P|
can't stop talking	:( )
Cartman	(((-_-)))
Cat in the Hat	||||8^)X
cheated, forlorn, sad	:-<
Chinese	<|-)
condescending	:-8(
confused and unhappy	%-(
confused but happy	%-)
confused but happy	%-<|>
constipated	|-/
couldn't care less	:o|
Count Dracula	(>:[X
critical, disgusted, determined, pouting	:-[
crying a lot	:~-(
crying a lot	&.(..
crying lots and lots	:~(~~
curly hair	&:-)
cursing, swearing	:-@
Daffy Duck	{:<>
dead	#-| #-(
dead	8-#
dead	X-(
dead	X-#
delicious, yummy	:-9
Devil	>:o)

devilish	}:-)
devilish	>:-)
devilish wink, lewd	;->
devilish, sarcastic	:->
disgusted (sticking out tongue)	:P
drooling	:-)~
drunk	%')
drunk	%-}
drunk	%*}
dunce	<:oO
ecstatic	:-))))))))
evil thought	>;-)
falling in love	(*_*)
feeling sick	:-(*)
female	>-
flirt	@;-)
forked tongue	:-h
forked tongue	:-W
forked tongue	:-w
Frankenstein	[:=l]
Fred Flintstone	___2_2222___
Fred Flintstone	7:n)
fresh	P-)
full glass	\~/
glass (of drink)	_/
glasses on forehead	8:-)
go forth and prosper [Vulcan salute]	-\V/
goatee	:-(>~
goatee	:o)}
got a bad cold	:~~)
got a cold	:-~)
got my hood up	(((o-o)))
grim	8^|
guffawing loudly	:-):-):-)
hair parted down the middle	{:-)

haircut, needs	(-)
hair-raising experience	=:-o
hair-raising experience	=(8-0)
happy and crying	:')
happy and crying	:'-)
happy, joking, smiling, satisfied	:)
happy, joking, smiling, satisfied	:-)
happy, joyful	:o)
Harry Potter	~8-)
Harry Potter	—,,,^..^,,,—
heart-broken	:-...
high five	^5
Homer Simpson	~(_8^(l)
hug [cyber hug]	(((((name))))
hugs and kisses	(( )):**
hungover	%-\
hungover	%-/
hungover	%*@:-)
imaginative	!:-)
imperial TIE fighter	(-o-)
impish	):-)
impressed	-]:-)[-
in love	8-]
in suspense	8-|
indifferent, apathetic	:-|
jaw hitting the ground with shock	:-]
joking	;o)
just happy	8->
Kenny	(((><)))
kiss	:-*
kiss	:-x
Klingon	>>>:-]
koala bear	@(*0*)@
laughing	:-D
leering	;-}

leering	>:->
leering, wry, tipsy	:-}
let's make babies	~~~~o
lips sealed	:-# :-X
lipstick	:-{}
Lisa Simpson	{8-)
lost a contact lens	.-(
lost a contact lens	loO
Maggie Simpson	[8-*
male	:-
Marge Simpson	@@@@8-)
me	(-_-)
me asleep	lo
Mickey Mouse	8(:-)
mixed up	:~/
monk	<:-|
moonie	(_._)
moustache	:o{)
moustache	:-{)
mouth open, shocked, awed, amazed	:-( )
mouth open, very surprised, amazed	:-O
Mr Spock	/:-|
mug (of coffee, beer)	(_)
mug of very hot coffee or tea	@[_]~~
night	+<#^v
not amused	:/)
not amused	%-{ :/)
not very clever	-0.06
not very clever	%-6
obnoxious, sarcastic	:-]
octopus	~//(^o^)/~/~
owl	(OvO)
perplexed, puzzled, confused	:-/
Pikachu	(o^-^o)
Pinocchio	:----)

Pokemon	(*-*)
popcorn	* * * *
Pope	+-(:-)>+
Pope	+0:-)
pretzels	&&&&
punched on the nose	:_(
punk	-:-)
punk	=:-)
puzzled, perplexed	:-|
revolted	|-p
rose	@}--\-,---
rose	@->-
rose	@--)--)(--
rude devil	};->
rude devil	>-)
rude suggestions	>;->
Rudolph the Rednosed Reindeer	3:*>
sad	(:-\ :-<
sad	%-{
sad	8^(
sad and crying	:' (
sad and crying	:'-(
sad, unhappy, dissatisfied	:o(
Santa Claus, Father Christmas	*<:-)
scared	(:+(
sceptical, undecided	:-\
screaming	:-@
scuba diver	.._(:)-)
scuba diver with a broken mask	.._( )-)
shocked, amazed, appalled	:-o
shouting	:@
singing	(^O^)
sleepy	(=_=)
smirking	:-,
smirking	;^)

smirking	;>)
smitten by Cupid's arrow	>-::-D
smoking	:-Q
smoking a pipe	:-?
sniggering	|-)
snoring	|^o
snoring	3-O
snoring, yawning	|-O
sour, exhausted	:-6
Starship *Enterprise*	0
Starship *Enterprise* firing phasers	=-0~~~~
Starship *Enterprise* firing photon torpedoes	=-0***
stoned	*-)
straight-faced	:-T
strange	*8((:
surprised	:-<>
surprised	=) 8-(
sworn to secrecy	:-x
sworn to secrecy, lips sealed	:-X
talking	:-v
tangled hair	#:oO
thumbs up	^
tipsy, drunk	:*}
tongue in cheek	:-J
tongue in cheek	;-P
tongue in cheek, clowning	:^)
tongue out, panting in anticipation	:-P
tongue-tied	:-&
toupee	{:-)
toupee blowing in the wind	}:-(
two noses	:=)
two noses and happy	:=)
two noses and sad	:=(
uh-oh; silent	:-0
unbelieving, couldn't care less	:-C

Uncle Sam	=l:-)=
unconscious	%+(
unconscious	X-)
unhappy, sad, dissatisfied, frowning	:(
unhappy, sad, dissatisfied, frowning	:-(
vampire	:-[
very happy	:-))
very revolted	l-P
very unhappy	:-c
very unhappy	(:-(
very unhappy	{:-{
waving goodbye	(;.;)/~
waving hello	(^.^)/
wavy hair parted on one side	?:o)
wearing bow tie	:-)8
wearing bowler hat	Cl:-)
wearing braces	:o#
wearing cap	d:-)
wearing fur hat	#:-)
wearing glasses	'\=o-o=/'
wearing glasses	8-)
wearing glasses	8o)
wearing helmet	(:-)
wearing sunglasses	B:-)
wearing sunglasses	B-)
wearing turban	@:-)
wearing walkman	[:-)
wide-eyed smile	8-)
winking	;)
winking	;-)
winking	'-)
wry	:-7
yelling	:-(O)

An A-to-Z of Textspeak

As with emoticons, many of the coinages used in Textspeak are never found in routine messaging, being artful creations devised just for fun to see how far this kind of approach can be developed. The system has not yet reached its limit, and is still accreting new abbreviations, so the following list, though representative, should not be seen as complete.

Receiving: Abbreviations to Meanings

?	what?
@	at
@coll, @Coll	at college
@hm, @HM	at home
@schl, @SCHL	at school
@wrk, @WRK	at work
1daful, 1DAFUL	wonderful
2	to, too, two
24/7	twenty-four hours a day, seven days a week
2b, 2B	to be
2bctnd, 2BCTND	to be continued
2d4, 2D4	to die for
2day, 2DAY	today
2g4u, 2G4U	too good for you
2ht2hndl, 2HT2HNDL	too hot to handle
2l8, 2L8	too late

2moro, 2MORO, 2MoRo	tomorrow
2nite, 2NITE	tonight
2wimc, 2WIMC	to whom it may concern
3sum, 3SUM	threesome
4	for, four
4e, 4E	forever
4ever, 4EVER	forever
4evryrs, 4EVRYRS	forever yours
4EvrYrs	forever yours
4yeo, 4YEO	for your eyes only
7k, 7K	sick
8	ate
a3, A3	anytime, anywhere, anyplace
aam, AAM	as a matter of fact
aamof, AAMOF	as a matter of fact
ab, AB	ah bless!
activ8, ACTIV8	activate
adctd2luv, ADCTD2LUV, ADctd2Luv	addicted to love
add, ADD	address
adn, ADN	any day now
afaik, AFAIK	as far as I know
afk, AFK	away from keyboard
aisb, AISB	as I said before
aka, AKA	also known as
aliwanisu, ALIWANISU, ALIWanIsU	all I want is you
aml, AML	all my love
anfscd, ANFSCD	and now for something completely different
anytng, ANYTNG	anything
asap, ASAP	as soon as possible
asl, ASL	age, sex, location
aslmh, ASLMH	age, sex, location, music, hobbies

atb, ATB	all the best
atm, ATM	at the moment
atw, ATW	at the weekend
awhfy?, AWHFY?	are we having fun yet?
ax, AX	across
ayor, AYOR	at your own risk
b, B	be/bee
b2, B2	back to
b2b, B2B	business to business
b4, B4	before
b4n, B4N	bye for now
bbfn, BBFN	bye bye for now
bbl, BBL	be back later
bbs, BBS	be back soon
bbsd, BBSD	be back soon darling
bcame, BCAME	became
bcbc, BCBC	beggars can't be choosers
bcnu, BCNU	be seeing you
bcum, BCUM	become
beg, BEG	big evil grin
bf, BF	boyfriend
bfd, BFD	big fucking deal
bfn, BFN	bye for now
bg, BG	big grin
bgwm, BGWM	be gentle with me
bion, BION	believe it or not
bka, BKA	better known as
bmgwl, BMGWL	busting my gut with laughter
bn, BN	been
bn, BN	being
brb, BRB	be right back
brt, BRT	be right there
bta, BTA	but then again
btdt, BTDT	been there, done that

btr, BTR	better
btw, BTW	by the way
bwd, BWD	backward
bwl, BWL	bursting with laughter
c, C	see
c zin, C ZIN	season
c%d, C%D	could
c%l, C%L	cool
c&g, C&G	chuckle and grin
ceo, CEO	chief executive
chln, CHLN	chilling
chlya, CHLYA, ChLYa	chill ya!
cid, CID	consider it done
cid, CID	crying in disgrace
cld9?, CLD9?	cloud 9?
cm, CM	call me
cmap, CMAP	cover my ass, partner
cmb, CMB	call me back
cn, CN	can
cnc, CNC, CnC	cheap and cheerful
cos, COS	because
cr8, CR8	create
crbt, CRBT	crying really big tears
csg, CSG	chuckle snicker grin
csthnknau, CSTHNKNAU, CSThnKnAU	can't stop thinking about you
cu, CU	see you
cu @ 8, CU @ 8 [etc.]	see you at 8 [etc.]
cu2moro, CU2MORO, CU2MoRo	see you tomorrow
cu2nite, CU2NITE	see you tonight
cuimd, CUIMD	see you in my dreams
cul, CUL	see you later
cul8r, CUL8R	see you later

cul8r alig8r n whl crcdl, CUL8R ALIG8R N WHL CRCDL, cul8r g8r n whl crcdl, CUL8R G8R N WHL CRCDL	see you later alligator, in a while crocodile
cunvr, CUNVR	see you never
cupl, CUPL	couple
cus, CUS	see you soon
cuz, CUZ	because
cw2cu, CW2CU	can't wait to see you
cya, CYA	cover your ass
cya, CYA	see ya
cyo, CYO	see you online
d, D	the
d8, D8	date
d8ing, D8ING	dating
db8, DB8	debate
dd, DD, Dd	dead
dict8, DICT8	dictate
dinr, DINR	dinner
dk, DK	don't know
dl, DL	download
dm&, DM&	demand
dndc, DNDC	don't know, don't care
doin, DOIN	doing
dom, DOM	dirty old man
dur, DUR	do you remember
dv8, DV8	deviate
dwb, DWB	don't write back
dxnre, DXNRE	dictionary
e2eg, E2EG	ear to ear grin
emsg, EMSG	email message
eod, EOD	end of discussion
eol, EOL	end of lecture
eta, ETA	estimated time of arrival

ezi, EZI	easy
ezy, EZY	easy
f?, F?	friends?
f2f, F2F	face-to-face
f2t, F2T	free to talk
faq, FAQ	frequently asked question/s
fawc, FAWC	for anyone who cares
fc, FC	fingers crossed
ficcl, FICCL	frankly, I couldn't care less
fitb, FITB	fill in the blank
foaf, FOAF	friend of a friend
fone, FONE	phone
fotcl, FOTCL	falling off the chair laughing
fst, FST	fast
ftasb, FTASB	faster than a speeding bullet
ftac, FTAC	fantasy
ftbl, FTBL, FtBl	football
fubar, FUBAR	fucking up beyond all repair or recognition
fune, FUNE, funE	funny
fwd, FWD	forward
fwiw, FWIW	for what it's worth
fya, FYA	for your amusement
fyi, FYI	for your information
g, G	grin
g2cu, G2CU	glad/good to see you
g2g, G2G	got to go
g2sy, G2SY	glad/good to see you
g9, G9	genius
gal, GAL	get a life
galgal, GALGAL	give a little, get a little
gbh, GBH	great big hug
gbh, GBH	grevious bodily harm
gd&r, GD&R	grinning, ducking and running

gf, GF	girlfriend
gg, GG	good game
ggfn, GGFN	got to go for now
ggp, GGP	got to go pee
gizza, GIZZA	give us a
gj, GJ	good job
gl, GL	good luck
gm, GM	good move
gmab, GMAB	give me a break
gmbo, GMBO	giggling my butt off
gmesumluvin, GMESUMLUVIN, GMeSumLuvin	give me some loving
gmta, GMTA	great minds think alike
gnr8, GNR8	generate
gnr8n, GNR8N	generation
gnrle, GNRLE	generally
gonna, GONNA	going to
gr8, GR8	great
grovbab, GROVBAB, GrOvBAB	groovy baby!
gsoh, GSOH	good salary, own home
gsoh, GSOH	good sense of humour
gt, GT	good try
gtcu, GTCU	glad/good to see you
gtg, GTG	got to go
gtsy, GTSY	glad/good to see you
h2cus, H2CUS	hope to see you soon
h8, H8	hate
habu, HABU	have a better 'un
hagn, HAGN	have a good night
hagu, HAGU	have a good 'un
hak, HAK	hugs and kisses
hamrd, HAMRD	hammered
hand, HAND	have a nice day

hbtu, HBTU	happy birthday to you
hdepiyluv?, HDEPIYLUV?, HDEpIYLuv?	how deep is your love?
hhoj, HHOJ	ha, ha only joking
hig, HIG?	how's it going?
hldmecls, HLDMECLS, HldMeCls	hold me close
hohil HOHIL	head over heels in love
hotluv, HOTLUV, HotLuv	hot love
hotx3, HOTX3	hot, hot, hot
howru?, HOWRU?, HowRu?	how are you?
ht4u, HT4U, Ht4U	hot for you
hth, HTH	hope this helps
humr, HUMR	humour
hv, HV	have
i, I	eye
iac, IAC	in any case
iae, IAE	in any event
ianal, IANAL	I'm not a lawyer, but . . .
ic, IC	I see
ic**wenuxme, IC**WENUXME, IC**WenUXMe	I see stars when you kiss me
iccl, ICCL	I couldn't care less
icq, ICQ	I seek you
icwum, ICWUM	I see what you mean
idk, IDK	I don't know
idkiukb, IDKIUKB	I don't know if you know but . . .
idlu, IDLU	I don't like you
igotubabe, IGOTUBABE, IGotUBabe	I've got you, babe
igp, IGP	I gotta pee
igpt, IGTP	I get the point

ih8u, IH8U	I hate you
iirc, IIRC	if I recall/remember correctly
ijc2sailuvu, IJC2SAILUVU, IJC2SaILuvU	I just called to say I love you
ilu, ILU	I love you
iluvu, ILUVU, IluvU	I love you
iluvu2, ILUVU2	I love you too
iluvumed, ILUVUMED, ILuvUMED	I love you more each day
ily, ILY	I love you
ily2, ILY2	I love you too
im, IM	I am
im, IM	immediate message
imbluv, IMBLUV, IMBLuv	it must be love
imco, IMCO	in my considered opinion
imhbco, IMHBCO	in my humble but correct opinion
imho, IMHO	in my honest/humble opinion
imi, IMI	I mean it
imnsho, IMNSHO	in my not so humble opinion
imo, IMO	in my opinion
imprs, IMPRS	impress
iohis4u, IOHIS4U, IOHis4U	I only have eyes for you
iooh, IOOH	I'm outta here
iou, IOU	I owe you
iounotn, IOUNOTN, IouNotn	I owe you nothing
iow, IOW	in other words
iowan2bwu, IOWAN2BWU, IOWan2BWU	I only want to be with you
irl, IRL	in real life
itigbs, ITIGBS	I think I'm gonna be sick

itufir, ITUFIR	I think you'll find I'm right
ityfir, ITYFIR	I think you'll find I'm right
iuss, IUSS	if you say so
iwalu, IWALU	I will always love you
iwanu, IWANU, IWanU	I want you
iwlalwysluvu, IWLALWYSLUVU, IWLAlwysLuvU	I will always love you
iydkidkwd, IYDKIDKWD	if you don't know, I don't know who does
iykwim, IYKWIM	if you know what I mean
iyss, IYSS	if you say so
j4f, J4F	just for fun
jam, JAM	just a minute
jas, JAS	just a second
jic, JIC	just in case
jk, JK	just kidding
jmo, JMO	just my opinion
jstcllme, JSTCLLME, JstCllMe	just call me
jtluk, JTLUK	just to let you know
jtlyk, JTLYK	just to let you know
kc, KC	keep cool
khuf, KHUF	know how you feel
kiss, KISS	keep it simple, stupid
kit, KIT	keep in touch
koc, KOC	kiss on cheek
kol, KOL	kiss on lips
kotc, KOTC	kiss on the cheek
kotl, KOTL	kiss on the lips
kwim, KWIM	know what I mean
l, L	laugh
l8, L8	late
l8r, L8R	later
l8r g8r, L8R G8R	later 'gator

lch, LCH	lunch
ldr, LDR	long-distance relationship
lhm, LHM	Lord help me
lhu, LHU	Lord help you
lkit, LKIT	like it
lmao, LMAO	laugh/laughing my ass off
lmk, LMK	let me know
lmso, LMSO	laugh/laughing my socks off
lngtmnoc, LNGTMNOC, LngTmNoC	long time no see
lo, LO	hello
lol, LOL	laugh/laughing out loud
lol, LOL	lots of love
lshmbb, LSHMBB	laughing so hard my belly is bouncing
lshmbh, LSHMBH	laughing so hard my belly hurts
ltnc, LTNC	long time no see
ltns, LTNS	long time no see
lts, LTS	laughing to self
ltsgt2gthr, LTSGT2GTHR, LtsGt2gthr	let's get together
luv, LUV	love
luvu, LUVU, LuvU	love you
luvya, LUVYA, LuvYa	love you
luwamh, LUWAMH	love you with all my heart
m8, M8	mate
mbrsd, MBRSD	embarrassed
mc, MC	Merry Christmas
md, MD	managing director
mfi, MFI	mad for it
mgb, MGB, mGb	may God bless
mmyt, MMYT	mail me your thoughts
mob, MOB	mobile

msg, MSG	message
msulkecrz, MSULKECRZ, MSULkeCrZ	miss you like crazy
mte, MTE	my thoughts exactly
mtf, MTF	more to follow
mtfbwu, MTFBWU	may the force be with you
myob, MYOB	mind your own business
n, N	and
n, N	no
n1, N1	nice one!
na, NA	no access
nagi, NAGI	not a good idea
nc, NC	no comment
ncase, NCASE	in case
ne, NE	any
ne1, NE1	anyone
ned, NED, nEd	need
nethng, NETHNG	anything
no1, NO1	no one
np, NP	no problem
nrn, NRN	no reply necessary
nt2nite, NT2NITE, Nt2Nite	not tonight
nvm, NVM	never mind
nwo, NWO	no way out
o, O	or
o ****, O ****	oh fuck!
o4u, O4U	only for you
obab, OBAB	oh baby
obtw, OBTW	oh by the way
ohmigod, OHMIGOD	oh my God
omigod, OMIGOD	oh my God
oic, OIC	oh I see
ol, OL	old lady
om, OM	old man
omg, OMG	oh my God

on 4it, ON4IT, On4It	on for it
otoh, OTOH	on the other hand
ott, OTT	over the top
ottomh, OTTOMH	off the top of my head
ova, OVA	over
pcm, PCM	please call me
pds, PDS	please don't shoot
pita, PITA	pain in the ass
pls, PLS	please
pls4givme, PLS4GIVME, Pls4GivMe	please forgive me
pm, PM	private message
pmji, PMJI	pardon my jumping in
pml, PML	pissing myself laughing
poahf, POAHF	put on a happy face
ppl, PPL	people
prt, PRT	party
prw, PRW	parents are watching
ptmm, PTMM	please tell me more
q, Q	queue
qix, QIX	quick
qpsa?, QPSA?	que pasa?
qt, QT	cutie
r, R	are
rad, RAD	radical
rgds, RGDS	regards
rip, RIP	rest in peace
rmb, RMB	ring my bell
rotfl, ROTFL	rolling on the floor laughing
rotflmao, ROTFLMAO	rolling on the floor laughing my ass off
rotflmaoay, ROTFLMAOAY	rolling on the floor laughing my ass off at you

rotflmaowtime, ROTFLMAOWTIME	rolling on the floor laughing my ass off with tears in my eyes
rotflol, ROTFLOL	rolling on the floor laughing out loud
rotfluts, ROTFLUTS	rolling on the floor laughing unable to speak
ruok?, RUOK?, RuOK?	are you OK?
rutlkn2me?, RUTLKN2ME?, RUTlkn2ME?	are you talking to me?
ruup4it?, RUUP4IT?, RUUp4it?	are you up for it?
sal, SAL	such a laugh
sc, SC	stay cool
sec, SEC	second
sete, SETE	smiling ear to ear
sit, SIT	stay in touch
sk8, SK8	skate
sme1, SME1	someone
smtoe, SMTOE	sets my teeth on edge
snafu, SNAFU	situation normal, all fouled up
snert, SNERT	snot-nosed egotistical rude teenager
so, SO	significant other
sohf, SOHF	sense of humour failure
sol, SOL	sooner or later
sot, SOT	short of time
sotmg, SOTMG	short of time must go
spk, SPK	speak
sry, SRY	sorry
st2moro, ST2MORO, ST2MoRo	same time tomorrow
stats, STATS	your sex and age [statistics]

stra, STRA	stray
stw, STW	search the web
suakm, SUAKM	shut up and kiss me
sum1, SUM1	someone
sup?, SUP?	what's up?
swak, SWAK	sealed with a kiss
swalk, SWALK	sealed with a loving kiss
swalk, SWALK	sent with a loving kiss
swdyt?, SWDYT?	so what do you think?
swg, SWG	scientific wild guess
swl, SWL	screaming with laughter
sys, SYS	see you soon
t+, T+	think positive
t2go, T2GO, T2Go	time to go
t2ul, T2UL	talk to you later
t2ul8r, T2UL8R	talk to you later
t2yl, T2YL	talk to you later
t2yl8r, T2YL8r	talk to you later
ta4n, TA4N	that's all for now
tafn, TAFN	that's all for now
tcoy, TCOY	take care of yourself
tdtu, TDTU	totally devoted to you
tel, TEL	telephone
thn, THN, thN	then
thnq, THNQ	thank you
thnx, THNX	thanks
thx, THX	thanks
tia, TIA	thanks in advance
tic, TIC	tongue in cheek
tmb, TMB	text me back
tmi, TMI	too much information
tmiy, TMIY	take me I'm yours
tmot, TMOT	trust me on this
tnt, TNT	till next time
tnx, TNX	thanks

topca, TOPCA	till our paths cross again
toy, TOY	thinking of you
truluv, TRULUV, TruLuv	true love
ttfn, TTFN	ta ta for now
tttt, TTTT	to tell the truth
ttul, TTUL	talk to you later
ttul8r, TTUL8R	talk to you later
ttutt, TTUTT	to tell you the truth
ttyl, TTYL	talk to you later
ttyl8r, TTYL8R	talk to you later
ttytt, TTYTT	to tell you the truth
tuvm, TUVM	thank you very much
tx, TX	thanks
txt, TXT	text
txtin, TXTIN	texting
u, U	you
u+me=luv, U+ME=LUV, U+ME=Luv	you and/plus me equals love
u2, U2	you too
u4e, U4E	yours forever
up4it, UP4IT	up for it
ur, UR	you are
urd1, URD1	you are the one
urhstry, URHSTRY, UrHStry	you are history!
urt1, URT1	you are the one
uwot, UWOT, Uwot	you what!
vgc, VGC	very good condition
vri, VRI	very
w, W	with
w/o, W/O	without
w4u, W4U	waiting for you
w8, W8	wait
w84me, W84ME, W84Me	wait for me
wadr, WADR	with all due respect

wan2, WAN2	want to
wan2tlk?, WAN2TLK?, Wan2Tlk?	want to talk?
wassup? WASSUP?	what's up?
wayd, WAYD?	what are you doing?
wb, WB	welcome back
wbs, WBS	write back soon
wckd, WCKD	wicked
wdalyic?, WDALYIC?	who died and left you in charge?
wen, WEN	when
wenja?, WENJA?	when do you?
werja?, WERJA?	where do you?
werru?, WERRU?, WerRU?	where are you?
werubn?, WERUBN?, WerUBn?	where have you been?
wfm, WFM	works for me
wk, WK	week
wknd, WKND	weekend
wl, WL	will
wlubmn?, WLUBMN?, WLUBMn?	will you be mine?
wlumryme?, WLUMRYME?, WLUMRyMe?	will you marry me?
wn, WN	when
wot, WOT	what
wrt, WRT	with respect to
wsuuuuu?, WSUUUUU?, WsUuuuu?	what's up?
wtf, WTF	what the fuck
wtfigo?, WTFIGO?	what the fuck is going on?
wtg, WTG	way to go
wth, WTH	what/who the heck
wtm?, WTM?	what time?

wu?, WU?	what's up?
wuf?, WUF?	where are you from?
wuwh, WUWH	wish you were here
wysiwyg, WYSIWYG	what you see is what you get
wywh, WYWH	wish you were here
x, X	kiss
x!, X!	typical woman
xclusvlyyrs, XCLUSVLYYRS, XclusvlyYrs	exclusively yours
xlnt, XLNT	excellent
xmeqk, XMEQK, XMeQk	kiss me quick
xoxoxo, XOXOXO	hugs and kisses
y, Y	why
y, Y	yes
y!, Y!	typical man
ya, YA	you
ya, YA	your
ybs, YBS	you'll be sorry
yg, YG	young gentleman
yiu, YIU	yes I understand
ykwycd, YKWYCD	you know what you can do
yl, YL	young lady
ym, YM	young man
yr, YR	your
yrplcomn?, YRPLCOMN?, YrPlcoMn?	your place or mine?
yyssw, YYSSW	yeah, yeah, sure, sure – whatever
z, Z	said
zzzz, ZZZZ	sleeping

Sending: Meanings to Abbreviations

across	ax, AX
activate	activ8, ACTIV8
addicted to love	adctd2luv, ADCTD2LUV, ADctd2Luv
address	add, ADD
age, sex, location	asl, ASL
ah bless!	ab, AB
all I want is you	aliwanisu, ALIWANISU, ALlWanIsU
all my love	aml, AML
all the best	atb, ATB
also known as	aka, AKA
and	n, N
any	ne, NE
any day now	adn, ADN
anyone	ne1, NE1
anything	anytng, ANYTNG, nethng, NETHNG
anytime, anywhere, anyplace	a3, A3
are	r, R
are we having fun yet?	awhfy?, AWHFY?
are you OK?	ruok?, RUOK?, RuOK?
are you talking to me?	rutlkn2me?, RUTLKN2ME?, RUTlkn2ME?
are you up for it?	ruup4it?, RUUP4IT?, RUUp4it?
as a matter of fact	aam, AAM, aamof, AAMOF
as far as I know	afaik, AFAIK
as I said before	aisb, AISB
as soon as possible	asap, ASAP
at	@
at college	@coll, @Coll

at home	@hm, @HM
at school	@schl, @SCHL
at the moment	atm, ATM
at the weekend	atw, ATW
at work	@wrk, @WRK
at your own risk	ayor, AYOR
ate	8
away from keyboard	afk, AFK
back to	b2, B2
backward	bwd, BWD
be/bee	b, B
be back later	bbl, BBL
be back soon	bbs, BBS
be back soon, darling	bbsd, BBSD
be gentle with me	bgwm, BGWM
be right back	brb, BRB
be right there	brt, BRT
be seeing you	bcnu, BCNU
became	bcame, BCAME
because	cos, COS, cuz, CUZ
become	bcum, BCUM
been	bn, BN
been there, done that	btdt, BTDT
before	b4, B4
beggars can't be choosers	bcbc, BCBC
being	bn, BN
believe it or not	bion, BION
better	btr, BTR
big evil grin	beg, BEG
big fucking deal	bfd, BFD
big grin	bg, BG
boyfriend	bf, BF
bursting with laughter	bwl, BWL
business to business	b2b, B2B

busting my gut with laughter	bmgwl, BMGWL
but then again	bta, BTA
by the way	btw, BTW
bye bye for now	bbfn, BBFN
bye for now	bfn, BFN, b4n, B4N
call me	cm, CM
call me back	cmb, CMB
can	cn, CN
can't stop thinking about you	csthnknau, CSTHNKNAU, CSThnKnAU
can't wait to see you	cw2cu, CW2CU
cheap and cheerful	cnc, CNC, CnC
chief executive	ceo, CEO
chill ya!	chlya, CHLYA, ChLYa
chilling	chln, CHLN
chuckle and grin	c&g, C&G
chuckle snicker grin	csg, CSG
cloud 9?	cld9?, CLD9?
consider it done	cid, CID
cool	c%l, C%L
could	c%d, C%D
couple	cupl, CUPL
cover my ass, partner	cmap, CMAP
cover your ass	cya, CYA
create	cr8, CR8
crying in disgrace	cid, CID
crying really big tears	crbt, CRBT
cutie	qt, QT
date	d8, D8
dating	d8ing, D8ING
dead	dd, DD, Dd
debate	db8, DB8
demand	dm&, DM&
deviate	dv8, DV8

dictate	dict8, DICT8
dictionary	dxnre, DXNRE
dinner	dinr, DINR
dirty old man	dom, DOM
do you remember	dur, DUR
doing	doin, DOIN
don't know	dk, DK
don't know, don't care	dndc, DNDC
don't write back	dwb, DWB
download	dl, DL
ear to ear grin	e2eg, E2EG
easy	ezi, EZI, ezy, EZY
email message	emsg, EMSG
embarrassed	mbrsd, MBRSD
end of discussion	eod, EOD
end of lecture	eol, EOL
estimated time of arrival	eta, ETA
excellent	xlnt, XLNT
exclusively yours	xclusvlyyrs, XCLUSVLYYRS, XclusvlyYrs
eye	i, I
fucking up beyond all repair or recognition	fubar, FUBAR
face-to-face	f2f, F2F
falling off the chair laughing	fotcl, FOTCL
fantasy	ftac, FTAC
fast	fst, FST
fill in the blank	fitb, FITB
fingers crossed	fc, FC
football	ftbl, FTBL, FtBl
for	4
forever	4e, 4E, 4ever, 4EVER
forever yours	4evryrs, 4EVRYRS, 4EvrYrs
for what it's worth	fwiw, FWIW
for your amusement	fya, FYA

for your eyes only	4yeo, 4YEO
for your information	fyi, FYI
forward	fwd, FWD
four	4
frankly, I couldn't care less	ficcl, FICCL
free to talk	f2t, F2T
frequently asked question/s	faq, FAQ
friends?	f?, F?
funny	fune, FUNE, funE
grin	g, G
generally	gnrle, GNRLE
generate	gnr8, GNR8
generation	gnr8n, GNR8N
genius	g9, G9
get a life	gal, GAL
giggling my butt off	gmbo, GMBO
girlfriend	gf, GF
give me a break	gmab, GMAB
give me some loving	gmesumluvin, GMESUMLUVIN, GMeSumLuvin
give us a	gizza, GIZZA
glad/good to see you	gtcu, GTCU, gtsy, GTSY, g2cu, G2CU, g2sy, G2SY
going to	gonna, GONNA
good game	gg, GG
good job	gj, GJ
good luck	gl, GL
good move	gm, GM
good salary, own home	gsoh, GSOH
good sense of humour	gsoh, GSOH
good try	gt, GT
got to go	gtg, GTG, g2g, G2G
got to go for now	ggfn, GGFN

got to go pee	ggp, GGP
great	gr8, GR8
great minds think alike	gmta, GMTA
grinning, ducking, and running	gd&r, GD&R
groovy baby!	grovbab, GROVBAB, GrOvBAB
ha, ha only joking	hhoj, HHOJ
hammered	hamrd, HAMRD
happy birthday to you	hbtu, HBTU
hate	h8, H8
have	hv, HV
have a better 'un	habu, HABU
have a good night	hagn, HAGN
have a good 'un	hagu, HAGU
have a nice day	hand, HAND
head over heels in love	hohil, HOHIL
hello	lo, LO
hold me close	hldmecls, HLDMECLS, HldMeCls
hope this helps	hth, HTH
hope to see you soon	h2cus, H2CUS
hot for you	ht4u, HT4U, Ht4U
hot love	hotluv, HOTLUV, HotLuv
hot, hot, hot	hotx3, HOTX3
how are you?	howru?, HOWRU?, HowRu?
how deep is your love?	hdepiyluv?, HDEPIYLUV?, HDEpIYLuv?
how's it going	hig, HIG
hugs and kisses	hak, HAK, xoxoxo, XOXOXO
humour	humr, HUMR
I am	im, IM
I couldn't care less	iccl, ICCL

I don't know	idk, IDK
I don't know if you know but . . .	idkiukb, IDKIUKB
I don't like you	idlu, IDLU
I gotta pee	igp, IGP
I hate you	ih8u, IH8U
I just called to say I love you	ijc2sailuvu, IJC2SAILUVU, IJC2SaILuvU
I love you	ilu, ILU, iluvu, ILUVU, IluvU, ily, ILY
I love you more each day	iluvumed, ILUVUMED, ILuvUMED
I love you too	iluvu2, ILUVU2, ily2, ILY2
I mean it	imi, IMI
I only have eyes for you	iohis4u, IOHIS4U, IOHis4U
I only want to be with you	iowan2bwu, IOWAN2BWU, IOWan2BWU
I owe you	iou, IOU
I owe you nothing	iounotn, IOUNOTN, IouNotn
I see	ic, IC
I see stars when you kiss me	ic**wenuxme, IC**WENUXME, IC**WenUXMe
I see what you mean	icwum, ICWUM
I seek you	icq, ICQ
I think I'm gonna be sick	itigbs, ITIGBS
I think you'll find I'm right	itufir, ITUFIR, ityfir, ITYFIR
I want you	iwanu, IWANU, IWanU
I will always love you	iwalu, IWALU, iwlalwysluvu, IWLALWYSLUVU, IWLAlwysLuvU

if I recall/remember correctly	iirc, IIRC
if you don't know, I don't know who does	iydkidkwd, IYDKIDKWD
if you know what I mean	iykwim, IYKWIM
if you say so	iuss, IUSS, iyss, IYSS
I'm not a lawyer, but . . .	ianal, IANAL
I'm outta here	iooh, IOOH
immediate message	im, IM
impress	imprs, IMPRS
in any case	iac, IAC
in any event	iae, IAE
in case	ncase, NCASE
in my considered opinion	imco, IMCO
in my honest/humble opinion	imho, IMHO
in my humble but correct opinion	imhbco, IMHBCO
in my not so humble opinion	imnsho, IMNSHO
in my opinion	imo, IMO
in other words	iow, IOW
in real life	irl, IRL
it must be love	imbluv, IMBLUV, IMBLuv
I've got you, babe	igotubabe, IGOTUBABE, IGotUBabe
just a minute	jam, JAM
just a second	jas, JAS
just call me	jstcllme, JSTCLLME, JstCllMe
just for fun	j4f, J4F
just in case	jic, JIC
just kidding	jk, JK
just my opinion	jmo, JMO
just to let you know	jtluk, JTLUK, jtlyk, JTLYK

keep cool	kc, KC
keep in touch	kit, KIT
keep it simple, stupid	kiss, KISS
kiss	x, X
kiss me quick	xmeqk, XMEQK, XMeQk
kiss on cheek	koc, KOC
kiss on lips	kol, KOL
kiss on the cheek	kotc, KOTC
kiss on the lips	kotl, KOTL
know how you feel	khuf, KHUF
know what I mean	kwim, KWIM
late	l8, L8
later	l8r, L8R
later 'gator	l8r g8r, L8R G8R
laugh	l, L
laugh/laughing my ass off	lmao, LMAO
laugh/laughing my socks off	lmso, LMSO
laugh/laughing out loud	lol, LOL
laughing so hard my belly hurts	lshmbh, LSHMBH
laughing so hard my belly is bouncing	lshmbb, LSHMBB
laughing to self	lts, LTS
let me know	lmk, LMK
let's get together	ltsgt2gthr, LTSGT2GTHR, LtsGt2gthr
like it	lkit, LKIT
long distance relationship	ldr, LDR
long time no see	lngtmnoc, LNGTMNOC, LngTmNoC, ltnc, LTNC, ltns, LTNS
Lord help me	lhm, LHM
Lord help you	lhu, LHU
lots of love	lol, LOL

love	luv, LUV
love you	luvu, LUVU, LuvU, luvya, LUVYA, LuvYa
love you with all my heart	luwamh, LUWAMH
lunch	lch, LCH
mad for it	mfi, MFI
mail me your thoughts	mmyt, MMYT
managing director	md, MD
mate	m8, M8
may God bless	mgb, MGB, mGb
may the force be with you	mtfbwu, MTFBWU
Merry Christmas	mc, MC
message	msg, MSG
mind your own business	myob, MYOB
miss you like crazy	msulkecrz, MSULKECRZ, MSULkeCrZ
mobile	mob, MOB
more to follow	mtf, MTF
my thoughts exactly	mte, MTE
need	ned, NED, nEd
never mind	nvm, NVM
nice one!	n1, N1
no	n, N
no access	na, NA
no comment	nc, NC
no one	no1, NO1
no problem	np, NP
no reply necessary	nrn, NRN
no way out	nwo, NWO
not a good idea	nagi, NAGI
not tonight	nt2nite, NT2NITE, Nt2Nite
off the top of my head	ottomh, OTTOMH
oh fuck!	o ****, O ****
oh baby	obab, OBAB
oh by the way	obtw, OBTW

oh I see	oic, OIC
oh my God	omg, OMG, ohmigod, OHMIGOD, omigod, OMIGOD
old lady	ol, OL
old man	om, OM
on for it	on4it, ON4IT, On4It
on the other hand	otoh, OTOH
only for you	o4u, O4U
or	o, O
over	ova, OVA
over the top	ott, OTT
pain in the ass	pita, PITA
pardon my jumping in	pmji, PMJI
parents are watching	prw, PRW
party	prt, PRT
people	ppl, PPL
phone	fone, FONE
pissing myself laughing	pml, PML
please	pls, PLS
please call me	pcm, PCM
please don't shoot	pds, PDS
please forgive me	pls4givme, PLS4GIVME, Pls4GivMe
please tell me more	ptmm, PTMM
private message	pm, PM
put on a happy face	poahf, POAHF
que pasa?	qpsa?, QPSA?
queue	q, Q
quick	qix, QIX
radical	rad, RAD
regards	rgds, RGDS
rest in peace	rip, RIP
ring my bell	rmb, RMB
rolling my eyes	rme, RME

rolling on the floor laughing	rotfl, ROTFL
rolling on the floor laughing my ass off	rotflmao, ROTFLMAO
rolling on the floor laughing my ass off at you	rotflmaoay, ROTFLMAOAY
rolling on the floor laughing my ass off with tears in my eyes	rotflmaowtime, ROTFLMAOWTIME
rolling on the floor laughing out loud	rotflol, ROTFLOL
rolling on the floor laughing unable to speak	rotfluts, ROTFLUTS
said	z, Z
same time tomorrow	st2moro, ST2MORO, ST2MoRo
scientific wild guess	swg, SWG
screaming with laughter	swl, SWL
sealed with a kiss	swak, SWAK
sealed with a loving kiss	swalk, SWALK
search the web	stw, STW
season	c zin, C ZIN
second	sec, SEC
see	c, C
see ya	cya, CYA
see you	cu, CU
see you at 8 [etc.]	cu @ 8, CU @ 8 [etc.]
see you in my dreams	cuimd, CUIMD
see you later	cul, CUL, cul8r, CUL8R
see you later alligator, in a while crocodile	cul8r alig8r n whl crcdl, CUL8R ALIG8R N WHL CRCDL
see you later 'gator, in a while crocodile	cul8r g8r n whl crcdl, CUL8R G8R N WHL CRCDL
see you never	cunvr, CUNVR

see you online	cyo, CYO
see you soon	cus, CUS, sys, SYS
see you tomorrow	cu2moro, CU2MORO, CU2MoRo
see you tonight	cu2nite, CU2NITE
sense of humour failure	sohf, SOHF
sent with a loving kiss	swalk, SWALK
sets my teeth on edge	smtoe, SMTOE
short of time	sot, SOT
short of time must go	sotmg, SOTMG
shut up and kiss me	suakm, SUAKM
sick	7k, 7K
significant other	so, SO
situation normal, all fouled up	snafu, SNAFU
skate	sk8, SK8
sleeping	zzzz, ZZZZ
smiling ear to ear	sete, SETE
snot-nosed egotistical rude teenager	snert, SNERT
so what do you think?	swdyt?, SWDYT?
someone	sme1, SME1, sum1, SUM1
sooner or later	sol, SOL
sorry	sry, SRY
speak	spk, SPK
stay cool	sc, SC
stay in touch	sit, SIT
stray	stra, STRA
such a laugh	sal, SAL
ta ta for now	ttfn, TTFN
take care of yourself	tcoy, TCOY
take me I'm yours	tmiy, TMIY

talk to you later	ttul, TTUL, ttul8r, TTUL8R, ttyl, TTYL, ttyl8r, TTYL8R, t2ul, T2UL, t2ul8r, T2UL8R, t2yl, T2YL, t2yl8r, T2YL8r
telephone	tel, TEL
text	txt, TXT
text me back	tmb, TMB
texting	txtin, TXTIN
thank you	thnq, THNQ
thank you very much	tuvm, TUVM
thanks	thnx, THNX, thx, THX, tnx, TNX, tx, TX
thanks in advance	tia, TIA
that's all for now	tafn, TAFN, ta4n, TA4N
the	d, D
then	thn, THN, thN
think positive	t+, T+
thinking of you	toy, TOY
threesome	3sum, 3SUM
till our paths cross again	topca, TOPCA
till next time	tnt, TNT
time to go	t2go, T2GO, T2Go
to, too, two	2
to be	2b, 2B
to be continued	2bctnd, 2BCTND
to die for	2d4, 2D4
to tell the truth	tttt, TTTT
to tell you the truth	ttutt, TTUTT, ttytt, TTYTT
to whom it may concern	2wimc, 2WIMC
today	2day, 2DAY
tomorrow	2moro, 2MORO, 2MoRo
tonight	2nite, 2NITE
too good for you	2g4u, 2G4U
too hot to handle	2ht2hndl, 2HT2HNDL

too late	2l8, 2L8
too much information	tmi, TMI
totally devoted to you	tdtu, TDTU
tongue in cheek	tic, TIC
true love	truluv, TRULUV, TruLuv
trust me on this	tmot, TMOT
twenty-four hours a day, seven days a week	24/7
typical man	y! Y!
typical woman	x! X!
up for it	up4it, UP4IT
very	vri, VRI
very good condition	vgc, VGC
wait	w8, W8
wait for me	w84me, W84ME, W84Me
waiting for you	w4u, W4U
want to	wan2, WAN2
want to talk?	wan2tlk?, WAN2TLK?, Wan2Tlk?
way to go	wtg, WTG
week	wk, WK
weekend	wknd, WKND
welcome back	wb, WB
what	wot, WOT
what	?
what are you doing?	wayd, WAYD?
what the fuck	wtf, WTF
what the fuck is going on?	wtfigo?, WTFIGO?
what time?	wtm?, WTM?
what you see is what you get	wysiwyg, WYSIWYG
what/who the heck	wth, WTH
what's up?	wassup?, WASSUP?, sup?, SUP?, wsuuuuu?, WSUUUUU?, WsUuuuu?, wu?, WU?

when	wen, WEN, wn, WN
when do you?	wenja?, WENJA?
where are you?	werru?, WERRU?, WerRU?
where are you from?	wuf?, WUF?
where do you?	werja?, WERJA?
where have you been?	werubn?, WERUBN?, WerUBn?
who died and left you in charge?	wdalyic?, WDALYIC?
why	y, Y
wicked	wckd, WCKD
will	wl, WL
will you be mine?	wlubmn?, WLUBMN?, WLUBMn?
will you marry me?	wlumryme?, WLUMRYME?, WLUMRyMe?
wish you were here	wuwh, WUWH, wywh, WYWH
with	w, W
with all due respect	wadr, WADR
with respect to	wrt, WRT
without	w/o, W/O
wonderful	1daful, 1DAFUL
works for me	wfm, WFM
write back soon	wbs, WBS
yeah, yeah, sure, sure – whatever	yyssw, YYSSW
yes	y, Y
yes I understand	yiu, YIU
you	u, U, ya, YA
you and me equals love	u+me=luv, U+ME=LUV, U+ME=Luv
you are	ur, UR

you are history!	urhstry, URHSTRY, UrHStry
you are the one	urt1, URT1
you know what you can do	ykwycd, YKWYCD
you plus me equals love	u+me=luv, U+ME=LUV, U+Me=Luv
you too	u2, U2
you what!	uwot, UWOT, Uwot
you'll be sorry	ybs, YBS
young gentleman	yg, YG
young lady	yl, YL
young man	ym, YM
your	ya, YA, yr, YR
you are the one	urd1, URD1
your place or mine?	yrplcomn?, YRPLCOMN?, YrPlcoMn?
your sex and age	stats, STATS
yours forever	u4e, U4E

An A-to-Z of
Internet Domain Names

Receiving: Abbreviations to Meanings

The Internet Corporation for Assigned Names and Numbers (ICANN) is a technical co-ordination body for the Internet, created in 1998. It took over responsibility for a set of technical functions previously performed under US Government contract by the Internet Assigned Numbers Authority (IANA) and other groups. Specifically, ICANN co-ordinates the assignment of the following identifiers that must be globally unique for the Internet to function:

- Internet domain names
- IP address numbers
- Protocol parameter and port numbers.

In addition, ICANN co-ordinates the stable operation of the Internet's root server system. Further information can be found at <www.icann.org>, and information about domain-name registration at Internic: <http://www.internic.net/faqs/domain-names.html>.

There are two main types of top-level domains (TLDs): *generic* and *country code*, plus a special top-level domain (.arpa) for Internet infrastructure (Address and Routing Parameter Area). Generic domains were created to be used by the Internet public, while country-code domains were created to be used by individual countries. The original set of generic codes was devised in 1988, and an additional set was given formal approval in 2000. Several other proposals are being discussed, such as .arts, .earth, .firm, .kidz, .law, .news, .sex, .shop and .store. Those in favour of new TLDs argue that they relieve the pressure on existing name spaces and promote consumer choice; those against point to such problems as increased consumer confusion and trademark infringement.

Generic Codes

GENERIC DOMAINS

.aero	Aviation
.biz	Business Organizations
.com	Commercial Enterprises
.coop	Co-operative Organizations
.edu	Educational
.gov	US Government
.info	Open top-level domain
.int	International Treaty Organizations
.mil	Dept of Defense (US)
.museum	Museums
.name	Personal Names
.net	Internet Service Provider
.org	Non-Commercial Organizations
.pro	Professionals (accountants, lawyers, physicians, etc.)

UK SECOND-LEVEL DOMAINS

Managed by Nominet

.co.uk	Commercial Enterprises
.ltd.uk	Registered Company Name
.me.uk	Personal
.net.uk	Internet Service Provider
.org.uk	Non-Commercial Organizations
.plc.uk	Registered Company Name
.sch.uk	Schools

Not managed by Nominet

.ac.uk	Academic Establishments
.gov.uk	Government Bodies

.mod	Ministry of Defence Establishments
.nhs	National Health Service
.police	Police Forces

Country Codes

ICANN uses a politically neutral list of two-letter codes maintained by the ISO 3166 Maintenance Agency. The management of the domain name within a region is in the hands of a local body registered for the purpose (such as Nominet in the UK). To be included in the list an applicant must be listed in the United Nations Terminology Bulletin *Country Names* or in the *Country and Region Codes for Statistical Use* of the UN Statistics Division. And to be listed in that bulletin, the applicant must be a member country of the United Nations, a member of one of its specialized agencies, or a party to the Statute of the International Court of Justice.

A few countries whose abbreviations permit a general interpretation (at least, in English) have entered into agreements their code to be used as a generic indicator. The code for Tuvalu, *tv*, is now widely used as a designator for sites related to television, but the lively semantic associations of the abbreviation have made it attractive to organizations that are not part of the television world (e.g. <www.findout.tv>). Other country sites which have achieved some degree of general functionality include *bz* (Belize), as an alternative for 'business', *ws* (Samoa) for 'website', and *cc* (Cocos Islands), offering a further option to anyone wanting to use a particular name where the more conventional codes are already being used.

.ac	Ascension Island
.ad	Andorra
.ae	United Arab Emirates
.af	Afghanistan
.ag	Antigua and Barbuda
.ai	Anguilla

.al	Albania
.am	Armenia
.an	Netherlands Antilles
.ao	Angola
.aq	Antarctica
.ar	Argentina
.as	American Samoa
.at	Austria
.au	Australia
.aw	Aruba
.az	Azerbaijan
.ba	Bosnia and Herzegovina
.bb	Barbados
.bd	Bangladesh
.be	Belgium
.bf	Burkina Faso
.bg	Bulgaria
.bh	Bahrain
.bi	Burundi
.bj	Benin
.bm	Bermuda
.bn	Brunei
.bo	Bolivia
.br	Brazil
.bs	Bahamas
.bt	Bhutan
.bv	Bouvet Island
.bw	Botswana
.by	Belarus
.bz	Belize
.ca	Canada
.cc	Cocos (Keeling) Islands
.cd	Congo, Democratic Republic of
.cf	Central African Republic
.cg	Congo

.ch	Switzerland
.ci	Côte d'Ivoire
.ck	Cook Islands
.cl	Chile
.cm	Cameroon
.cn	China
.co	Colombia
.cr	Costa Rica
.cs	Czechoslovakia (former state)
.cu	Cuba
.cv	Cape Verde
.cx	Christmas Island
.cy	Cyprus
.cz	Czech Republic
.de	Germany
.dj	Djibouti
.dk	Denmark
.dm	Dominica
.do	Dominican Republic
.dz	Algeria
.ec	Ecuador
.ee	Estonia
.eg	Egypt
.eh	Western Sahara
.er	Eritrea
.es	Spain
.et	Ethiopia
.fi	Finland
.fj	Fiji
.fk	Falkland Islands
.fm	Micronesia, Federated States of
.fo	Faroe Islands
.fr	France
.ga	Gabon
.gb	Great Britain

.gd	Grenada
.ge	Georgia
.gf	French Guiana
.gg	Guernsey
.gh	Ghana
.gi	Gibraltar
.gl	Greenland
.gm	Gambia, The
.gp	Guadeloupe
.gq	Equatorial Guinea
.gr	Greece
.gs	South Georgia and South Sandwich Islands
.gt	Guatemala
.gu	Guam
.gw	Guinea-Bissau
.gy	Guyana
.hk	Hong Kong
.hm	Heard and McDonald Islands
.hn	Honduras
.hr	Croatia
.ht	Haiti
.hu	Hungary
.id	Indonesia
.ie	Ireland
.il	Israel
.im	Isle of Man
.in	India
.io	British Indian Ocean Territory
.iq	Iraq
.ir	Iran
.is	Iceland
.it	Italy
.je	Jersey
.jm	Jamaica
.jo	Jordan

.jp	Japan
.ke	Kenya
.kg	Kyrgyzstan
.kh	Cambodia
.ki	Kiribati
.km	Comoros
.kn	Saint Kitts-Nevis
.kp	Korea, North
.kr	Korea, South
.kw	Kuwait
.ky	Cayman Islands
.kz	Kazakhstan
.la	Laos
.lb	Lebanon
.lc	Saint Lucia
.li	Liechtenstein
.lk	Sri Lanka
.lr	Liberia
.ls	Lesotho
.lt	Lithuania
.lu	Luxembourg
.lv	Latvia
.ly	Libya
.ma	Morocco
.mc	Monaco
.md	Moldova
.mg	Madagascar
.mh	Marshall Islands
.mk	Macedonia
.ml	Mali
.mm	Myanmar
.mn	Mongolia
.mo	Macau
.mp	Northern Mariana Islands
.mq	Martinique

.mr	Mauritania
.ms	Montserrat
.mt	Malta
.mu	Mauritius
.mv	Maldives
.mw	Malawi
.mx	Mexico
.my	Malaysia
.mz	Mozambique
.na	Namibia
.nc	New Caledonia
.ne	Niger
.nf	Norfolk Island
.ng	Nigeria
.ni	Nicaragua
.nl	Netherlands, The
.no	Norway
.np	Nepal
.nr	Nauru
.nu	Niue
.nz	New Zealand
.om	Oman
.pa	Panama
.pe	Peru
.pf	French Polynesia
.pg	Papua New Guinea
.ph	Philippines
.pk	Pakistan
.pl	Poland
.pm	St Pierre et Miquelon
.pn	Pitcairn Islands
.pr	Puerto Rico
.ps	Palestine
.pt	Portugal
.pw	Palau (Belau)

.py	Paraguay
.qa	Qatar
.re	Réunion
.ro	Romania
.ru	Russia
.rw	Rwanda
.sa	Saudi Arabia
.sb	Solomon Islands
.sc	Seychelles
.sd	Sudan
.se	Sweden
.sg	Singapore
.sh	St Helena
.si	Slovenia
.sj	Svalbard and Jan Mayen Islands
sk	Slovak Republic
.sl	Sierra Leone
.sm	San Marino
.sn	Senegal
.so	Somalia
.sr	Surinam
.st	São Tomé and Príncipe
.su	former Soviet Union (USSR)
.sv	El Salvador
.sy	Syria
.sz	Swaziland
.tc	Turks and Caicos Islands
.td	Chad
.tf	French Southern and Antarctic Territories
.tg	Togo
.th	Thailand
.tj	Tajikistan
.tk	Tokelau
.tm	Turkmenistan
.tn	Tunisia

.to	Tonga
.tp	East Timor
.tr	Turkey
.tt	Trinidad and Tobago
.tv	Tuvalu
.tw	Taiwan
.tz	Tanzania
.ua	Ukraine
.ug	Uganda
.uk	United Kingdom
.um	United States Minor Outlying Islands
.us	United States of America
.uy	Uruguay
.uz	Uzbekistan
.va	Vatican City
.vc	St Vincent and the Grenadines
.ve	Venezuela
.vg	Virgin Islands, British
.vi	Virgin Islands, United States
.vn	Vietnam
.vu	Vanuatu
.wf	Wallis and Futuna Islands
.ws	Samoa
.ye	Yemen
.yt	Mayotte
.yu	Yugoslavia (now Serbia and Montenegro)
.za	South Africa
.zm	Zambia
.zr	former Zaire (see Congo)
.zw	Zimbabwe

Sending: Meanings to Abbreviations

Generic Codes

GENERIC DOMAINS

Aviation	.aero
Business Organizations	.biz
Commercial Enterprises	.com
Co-operative Organizations	.coop
Dept of Defense (US)	.mil
Educational	.edu
International Treaty Organizations	.int
Internet Service Provider	.net
Museums	.museum
Non-Commercial Organizations	.org
Open top-level domain	.info
Personal Names	.name
Professionals (accountants, lawyers, physicians, etc.)	.pro
US Government	.gov

UK SECOND-LEVEL DOMAINS

Academic Establishments	.ac.uk
Commercial Enterprises	.co.uk
Government Bodies	.gov.uk
Internet Service Provider	.net.uk
Ministry of Defence Establishments	.mod
National Health Service	.nhs
Non-Commercial Organizations	.org.uk
Personal	.me.uk
Police Forces	.police
Registered Company Name	.ltd.uk
	.plc.uk
Schools	.sch.uk

Country Codes

Afghanistan	.af
Albania	.al
Algeria	.dz
American Samoa	.as
Andorra	.ad
Angola	.ao
Anguilla	.ai
Antarctica	.aq
Antigua and Barbuda	.ag
Argentina	.ar
Armenia	.am
Aruba	.aw
Ascension Island	.ac
Australia	.au
Austria	.at
Azerbaijan	.az
Bahamas	.bs
Bahrain	.bh
Bangladesh	.bd
Barbados	.bb
Belarus	.by
Belau	.pw
Belgium	.be
Belize	.bz
Benin	.bj
Bermuda	.bm
Bhutan	.bt
Bolivia	.bo
Bosnia and Herzegovina	.ba
Botswana	.bw
Bouvet Island	.bv
Brazil	.br
British Indian Ocean Territory	.io
Brunei	.bn

Bulgaria	.bg
Burkina Faso	.bf
Burundi	.bi
Cambodia	.kh
Cameroon	.cm
Canada	.ca
Cape Verde	.cv
Cayman Islands	.ky
Central African Republic	.cf
Chad	.td
Chile	.cl
China	.cn
Christmas Island	.cx
Cocos (Keeling) Islands	.cc
Colombia	.co
Comoros	.km
Congo	.cg
Congo, Democratic Republic of	.cd
Cook Islands	.ck
Costa Rica	.cr
Côte d'Ivoire	.ci
Croatia	.hr
Cuba	.cu
Cyprus	.cy
Czechoslovakia (former state)	.cs
Czech Republic	.cz
Denmark	.dk
Djibouti	.dj
Dominica	.dm
Dominican Republic	.do
East Timor	.tp
Ecuador	.ec
Egypt	.eg
El Salvador	.sv
Equatorial Guinea	.gq

Eritrea	.er
Estonia	.ee
Ethiopia	.et
Falkland Islands	.fk
Faroe Islands	.fo
Fiji	.fj
Finland	.fi
France	.fr
French Guiana	.gf
French Polynesia	.pf
French Southern and Antarctic Territories	.tf
Gabon	.ga
Gambia, The	.gm
Georgia	.ge
Germany	.de
Ghana	.gh
Gibraltar	.gi
Great Britain	.gb
Greece	.gr
Greenland	.gl
Grenada	.gd
Guadeloupe	.gp
Guam	.gu
Guatemala	.gt
Guernsey	.gg
Guinea-Bissau	.gw
Guyana	.gy
Haiti	.ht
Heard and McDonald Islands	.hm
Honduras	.hn
Hong Kong	.hk
Hungary	.hu
Iceland	.is
India	.in
Indonesia	.id

Iran	.ir
Iraq	.iq
Ireland	.ie
Isle of Man	.im
Israel	.il
Italy	.it
Jamaica	.jm
Japan	.jp
Jersey	.je
Jordan	.jo
Kazakhstan	.kz
Kenya	.ke
Kiribati	.ki
Korea, North	.kp
Korea, South	.kr
Kuwait	.kw
Kyrgyzstan	.kg
Laos	.la
Latvia	.lv
Lebanon	.lb
Lesotho	.ls
Liberia	.lr
Libya	.ly
Liechtenstein	.li
Lithuania	.lt
Luxembourg	.lu
Macau	.mo
Macedonia	.mk
Madagascar	.mg
Malawi	.mw
Malaysia	.my
Maldives	.mv
Mali	.ml
Malta	.mt
Marshall Islands	.mh

Martinique	.mq
Mauritania	.mr
Mauritius	.mu
Mayotte	.yt
Mexico	.mx
Micronesia, Federated States of	.fm
Moldova	.md
Monaco	.mc
Mongolia	.mn
Montserrat	.ms
Morocco	.ma
Mozambique	.mz
Myanmar	.mm
Namibia	.na
Nauru	.nr
Nepal	.np
Netherlands, The	.nl
Netherlands Antilles	.an
New Caledonia	.nc
New Zealand	.nz
Nicaragua	.ni
Niger	.ne
Nigeria	.ng
Niue	.nu
Norfolk Island	.nf
Northern Mariana Islands	.mp
Norway	.no
Oman	.om
Pakistan	.pk
Palau	.pw
Palestine	.ps
Panama	.pa
Papua New Guinea	.pg
Paraguay	.py
Peru	.pe

Philippines	.ph
Pitcairn Islands	.pn
Poland	.pl
Portugal	.pt
Puerto Rico	.pr
Qatar	.qa
Réunion	.re
Romania	.ro
Russia	.ru
Rwanda	.rw
Saint Helena	.sh
Saint Kitts-Nevis	.kn
Saint Lucia	.lc
Saint Pierre et Miquelon	.pm
Saint Vincent and the Grenadines	.vc
Samoa	.ws
San Marino	.sm
São Tomé and Príncipe	.st
Saudi Arabia	.sa
Senegal	.sn
Serbia and Montenegro	.yu
Seychelles	.sc
Sierra Leone	.sl
Singapore	.sg
Slovak Republic	sk
Slovenia	.si
Solomon Islands	.sb
Somalia	.so
South Africa	.za
South Georgia and South Sandwich Islands	.gs
Soviet Union (USSR), former	.su
Spain	.es
Sri Lanka	.lk
Sudan	.sd
Surinam	.sr

Svalbard and Jan Mayen Islands	.sj
Swaziland	.sz
Sweden	.se
Switzerland	.ch
Syria	.sy
Taiwan	.tw
Tajikistan	.tj
Tanzania	.tz
Thailand	.th
Togo	.tg
Tokelau	.tk
Tonga	.to
Trinidad and Tobago	.tt
Tunisia	.tn
Turkey	.tr
Turkmenistan	.tm
Turks and Caicos Islands	.tc
Tuvalu	.tv
Uganda	.ug
Ukraine	.ua
United Arab Emirates	.ae
United Kingdom	.uk
United States Minor Outlying Islands	.um
United States of America	.us
Uruguay	.uy
Uzbekistan	.uz
Vanuatu	.vu
Vatican City	.va
Venezuela	.ve
Vietnam	.vn
Virgin Islands, British	.vg
Virgin Islands, United States	.vi
Wallis and Futuna Islands	.wf
Western Sahara	.eh
Yemen	.ye

Yugoslavia (former)	.yu
Zaire, former (see Congo)	.zr
Zambia	.zm
Zimbabwe	.zw